Let Go
of Anger
& Stress!

"When I read Gary Zimak, I feel like I'm sitting in his living room sharing a cup of coffee and good conversation. His honesty and homespun wisdom are so refreshing. If you struggle with anger and stress (and who among us doesn't?), sit back and relax with Gary and be transformed!"

Gus Lloyd
Host of *Seize the Day*

"Gary Zimak's book is clear and well written. He writes about the Holy Spirit, not in celestial terms, but in practical, everyday, real life terms. Reading this book will illumine you with grace and change you!"

Rev. Cedric Pisegna, C.P.
Speaker, author, and TV host

"There's a Holy Spirit–led shift happening in our Church when it comes to discussing mental health and wellness, and Gary Zimak has entered that discussion with thoughtfulness and compassion. Filled with great ideas, questions for contemplation, and an open and vulnerable spirit, *Let Go of Anger and Stress!* is a blessing to those of us who often feel like we need to move toward God's peace but don't know where to start."

Tommy Tighe
Clinical counselor, Catholic author, and creator of the *St. Dymphna's Playbook* podcast

"Gary Zimak's relatable and disarming style makes this take on the Fruits of the Spirit an engaging resource for anyone who wants to cultivate the work of the Holy Spirit in their lives. Words such as *love, joy,* and *peace* are tossed around so often that the meaning is often lost; Gary gets to the heart of them with simple, practical, and profound reflections on how to live as disciples of Jesus. A great read for personal or group study!"

Matt Swaim
Cohost of *The Son Rise Morning Show*
Producer of *The Journey Home*

"This book is a strong call to each of us to follow the Lord more closely every day as he forms us into his likeness. Candor, wisdom, and practical, doable steps mark this book. Humor and love resonate through every page. Well done!"

Sr. Ann Shields, S.G.L.
Catholic speaker, author, and host of *Food for the Journey*

"*Let Go of Anger and Stress!* is a read worthy of your time and investment. Who wouldn't want to experience this transformation? This book can make a difference in your life."

David Mangan
Author of *God Loves You and There's Nothing You Can Do about It*

GARY ZIMAK

Author of *Give Up Worry for Lent!*

Let Go of Anger & Stress!

BE TRANSFORMED BY
THE FRUITS OF THE SPIRIT

AVE MARIA PRESS AVE Notre Dame, Indiana

Founded in 1865, Ave Maria Press is a ministry of the United States Province of Holy Cross.

www.avemariapress.com

Paperback: ISBN-13 978-1-59471-983-7

E-book: ISBN-13 978-1-59471-984-4

Cover image © gettyimages.com

Cover and text design by Brian C. Conley.

Printed and bound in the United States of America.

Library of Congress Cataloging-in-Publication Data
Names: Zimak, Gary, author.
Title: Let go of anger and stress! : be transformed by the fruits of the
   Spirit / Gary Zimak.
Description: Notre Dame, Indiana : Ave Maria Press, 2020. | Summary: "Gary
   Zimak reveals how cooperating with the Holy Spirit to cultivate seeds of
   virtue can bring victory over sinful habits-and result in a life of
   faith, joy, and personal holiness"-- Provided by publisher.
Identifiers: LCCN 2020020145 | ISBN 9781594719837 (paperback) | ISBN
   9781594719844 (ebook)
Subjects: LCSH: Fruit of the Spirit. | Holy Spirit. | Anger--Religious
   aspects--Christianity. | Habit breaking--Religious
   aspects--Christianity.
Classification: LCC BV4501.3 .Z55 2020 | DDC 234/.13--dc23
LC record available at https://lccn.loc.gov/2020020145

This book is dedicated to Fr. David Jakubiec, O.F.M. (1943–1988), and Ray Smith. Thank you for teaching me that Jesus is real and for introducing me to the Holy Spirit. I am extremely grateful.

Contents

Introduction

A violent squall came up and waves were breaking over the boat, so that it was already filling up. Jesus was in the stern, asleep on a cushion.
—Mark 4:37–38

Jesus was fast asleep. Even though he was in a boat battered by crashing waves and heavy winds, his companions convinced that they were all about to die, Jesus was asleep on a cushion in the stern. This was obviously one heck of a storm, but Jesus rested comfortably while seasoned fishermen panicked.

Wouldn't it be great if we could learn to react like Jesus when we are battered by the storms of life? For close to ten years, I have traveled around the country, leading parish missions and giving talks designed to help people find a closer relationship with Jesus Christ. In my presentations, I always make the point that the Lord wants to be involved in our lives and assist us with our daily struggles. With his help, it is possible to remain peaceful in the storm.

As I interact with fellow Catholics at my speaking engagements, I keep hearing the same comments:

> "How can I not stress out when the world is so crazy?"

> "I pray and go to Mass, but I'm still afraid."

> "I try not to get mad, but those people make me so angry!"

> "Worrying is part of life. I've just learned to accept it."

> "God is not answering my prayers and I'm tired of waiting!"

Many churchgoing Christians seem to believe that most problems we face each day are outside of God's jurisdiction. As a result, they live like practical atheists, as if God doesn't exist. They accept worry, hopelessness, misery, and hatred as a normal part of life. They fly off the handle and lose composure on a regular basis. For many people, "church life" and "real life" are totally separate.

Why does this happen? For the most part, it occurs when we lose sight of four important pieces of information:

- *The invisible world exists.* There is more to the world than what we perceive with our senses. Just because we can't see God doesn't mean that he doesn't exist. The same applies to the angels, and even to Satan. To experience peace and confidence in God (and share them with others), we first need to acknowledge that he is real. To combat the temptations of Satan, we must understand that he exists and that he's out to get us.

- *God is in control.* No matter what happens, God is always in control. The Bible tells us that it is God "whose hand holds the depths of the earth; who owns the tops of the mountains. The sea and dry land belong to God, who made them, formed them by hand" (Ps 95:4–5). We can't always see the solution to our problems from our limited perspective, but "nothing will be impossible for God" (Lk 1:37). God is much bigger than our problems and has given us everything we need to remain calm and to trust, if we open ourselves to those graces.

- *God loves us.* In the midst of turmoil, we often assume that God does not care about our struggles. Jesus experienced this firsthand with Martha (Lk 10:40) and the storm-battered apostles (Mk 4:38). Lashing out at God may be a natural human response in our difficulties, but it's not based on reality. According to the Bible, "God so loved the world that he gave his only Son, so that everyone who believes in him might not perish but might have eternal life" (Jn 3:16). He really does care!

- *God wants us to be at peace.* I often open my talks with the words "I want you to be free from anxieties." After the members of the audience smile and nod their heads, I let them know that I borrowed those words from St. Paul. In 1 Corinthians 7:32, the Holy Spirit inspired Paul to write that exact message. Guess what? If God wants you to be at peace, and free from all the effects of anger and stress, it must be possible. He would never ask you to do something that isn't possible. Unless you grasp that concept, you will never find the peace you seek.

SECRET WEAPONS OF FAITH

In this book, we will look at a variety of stress-producing situations and discover how the fruits of the Spirit—the cultivated harvest of the seeds of virtue planted inside us at Baptism, the "first fruits of eternal glory" (*CCC* 1832)—enable us to respond in a Christlike manner.

We will examine each of the fruits and explore ways to activate them in our lives. This approach doesn't involve ignoring the problems that surround us. Rather, it requires shifting focus, recognizing that God is always in charge and has given us these "secret weapons" of the faith, which the Spirit wants to help us use every day.

What are they, you ask? We can find both the "fruits of the flesh" and the "fruits of the Spirit" in St. Paul's letter to the Galatians:

> Now the works of the flesh are plain: immorality, impurity, licentiousness, idolatry, sorcery, enmity, strife, jealousy, anger, selfishness, dissension, party spirit, envy, drunkenness, carousing, and the like. I warn you . . . those who do such things shall not inherit the kingdom of God.
>
> But the fruit of the Spirit is love, joy, peace, patience, kindness, goodness, faithfulness, gentleness, self-control; against such there is no law. (Gal 5:19–23, RSVCE)

Take a moment and read this passage again slowly. Do any of these fleshly fruits give you trouble? Are there fruits of the Spirit that you find attractive, that you need to cultivate in your life? Then you've picked the right book—keep reading!

Each time we remove the fleshly fruits from our lives and ask the Holy Spirit to replace them with the fruit of the Spirit, good things happen. Not only will behaving in this way bring us peace, but it will also bring peace to those around us. It might not happen overnight, but we will gradually become more like Jesus, who slept during a raging storm. Aside from giving us the peace we seek, this new way of life also enables us to change our crazy world for the better!

A WORD OF CAUTION

Most of us know instinctively what we should and shouldn't do. We have the Bible and two thousand years of Church teaching to assist us in living holy, peaceful lives. (Even those who aren't very familiar with the Bible or the *Catechism of the Catholic Church* are often aware of the basic teachings of Jesus: pray, avoid worry, and repay hatred with love.) But how many times do even these basics trip us up? Why is it so difficult to follow his instructions?

Even though we know what we *should* do, our response to stressful situations is often the exact opposite of what Jesus commanded. We grow impatient and forget about praying as we run around trying to fix our problems on our own. We act as though everything depends on us. We think that we have to get things under control—and it has to be done *now*!

Before long, we become aware of our limitations and give in to worry and anger. Trying to relieve our stress, we turn to the internet, TV, or self-medication. Instead of helping, these activities often make us feel worse. Anxious and over-whelmed, we take out our frustration on those around us.

As Christians, shouldn't we be able to live peaceful lives and not fall apart when problems arise? Yes, but it's not quite that simple.

Even if we are aware of what Jesus said and what the Church teaches, we can't simply will ourselves to overcome these challenges. On our own, we will fail every time—especially when faced with a crisis or volatile situation. It's too easy to spin out of control. We need more than the Bible or the *Catechism* to help us deal with the challenges of daily life. These resources are important, but they are not enough.

Jesus knew that we would need additional help, and that's why he gave us the Holy Spirit, who plants within us tiny weapons of goodness—fruits, we call them—that we cultivate over the course of our lifetime. And that's what this book is all about.

LISTEN TO THE SPIRIT

Learning to follow the lead of the Holy Spirit is the secret to finding the peace you seek and living the life that God planned for you. Listening to the Spirit lets you know what to do and when to do it. His gentle voice will instruct you when to take action and when to rest in the Lord and wait. Instead of gritting your teeth and trying to remain calm in the face of adversity, follow the promptings of the Holy Spirit, and he will fill your heart with joy and peace.

Jesus never expected you to handle the struggles of life on your own. That's why the very Spirit (who guided him as he dealt with hostility and persecution) comes to live in you at

Baptism and wants to assist you every day. When Jesus said, "Do not worry about your life" (Mt 6:25), he knew that he would be sending someone to guide you. With the assistance of the Holy Spirit, it is possible to remain calm and in control in the middle of the storm.

By the time you reach the end of this book, you will learn how simple it is to unleash the power of the Holy Spirit in your life. It all starts with a powerful three-word prayer that should flow from your lips frequently. It's a prayer that will put you on the road to peace by letting the Holy Spirit work freely in your life. Do you long for the peace of Christ to dwell in your heart and spill over into all areas of your life? If so, let's begin our journey by praying this brief prayer. Don't be fooled by its simplicity. There is power in these three words. Repeat after me . . .

Come, Holy Spirit!

You may not realize it, but something just happened when you prayed those words. Even if you felt nothing, that simple prayer is always effective. When you invite the Holy Spirit to go to work in your life, fasten your seat belt and get ready. You're in for a wonderful and exciting journey. He will always respond.

Before too long, you'll find yourself able to rest comfortably even during the storm. Be patient and let the Holy Spirit gradually transform you into the image of Jesus. That's *his* job, and he does it well. Your job is to be docile and let him work in your life. If you can do that, you will be *transformed*!

> And we all, with unveiled face, beholding the glory of the Lord, are being changed into his likeness from one degree of glory to another; for this comes from the Lord who is the Spirit.
>
> —**2 Corinthians 3:18, RSVCE**

Part I

Laying the Foundation

1

Bring On the Power!

**But you will receive power when the holy Spirit
comes upon you.
—Acts 1:8**

Jesus spoke these words of consolation and promise to the
apostles and by extension to us, yet they are ignored by millions of Christians every day.

In all fairness, it's easy to see why. Jesus promising the
Holy Spirit to the early Church seems like old news, something that happened long ago. The only time this message
typically resonates with us is on Pentecost Sunday. One day
each year, we recall that the Holy Spirit descended on the
Church and something special happened. In a few hours,
however, we forget all about it. (But we shouldn't.)

Unfortunately, the significance of the word translated into
English as "power" is often lost on us—it is simply overused.
A baseball player who hits lots of home runs is referred to
as a "power hitter," a short rest is called a "power nap," and
a midday meeting between politicians or businesspeople is
sometimes known as a "power lunch." We speak of "powerful"

movies, songs, or plays. The word is used so casually that it doesn't seem like a big deal. Is it any surprise that Jesus' promise of power (courtesy of the Holy Spirit) is overlooked?

To better understand what Jesus was promising, we need to dig deeper.

FEEL THE POWER!

The New Testament was originally written in Greek, and certain words and phrases aren't easily translated into English. What exactly did St. Luke mean when he used the word "power" (*dunamis*) in Acts 1:8? This Greek word is the root of the English words "dynamite" and "dynamic." The kind of power Jesus promised was explosive!

When the Holy Spirit descended on the men and women of the early Church, they received explosive energy that changed their lives dramatically. The members of the early Church experienced radical conversion (we can read about it in the Acts of the Apostles), turning from their old ways and living together in peace, hope, and joy—often despite tremendous persecution and turmoil. They spoke in tongues, performed miraculous healings, and willingly put their lives in jeopardy to proclaim the Gospel so forcefully that thousands were drawn to the faith (despite the threat of persecution).

All of this was possible because of the Holy Spirit. Wouldn't it be great if we had access to that same kind of power? It would come in handy as we attempt to deal with the craziness going on in the world and in our lives. Here's some good news. Not only do we have access to that same power, but it is available to us *right now*!

COME, HOLY SPIRIT!

We first receive the Holy Spirit at Baptism, according to the *Catechism:* "Baptism not only purifies from all sins, but also makes the neophyte 'a new creature,' an adopted son of God, who has become a 'partaker of the divine nature,' member of Christ and co-heir with him, and a temple of the Holy Spirit" (*CCC* 1265).

The power of the Holy Spirit in us is then strengthened through the sacrament of Confirmation: "For by the sacrament of Confirmation, [the baptized] are more perfectly bound to the Church and are enriched with a special strength of the Holy Spirit. Hence they are, as true witnesses of Christ, more strictly obliged to spread and defend the faith by word and deed" (*CCC* 1285).

If you have been baptized and confirmed, you possess the same Holy Spirit given to the members of the early Church at the first Pentecost. You have all of the gifts (wisdom, understanding, counsel, fortitude, knowledge, piety, and fear of the Lord), and you have the "power"! Do you feel it? If not, you're not alone.

When faced with the struggles of life, even loyal followers of Christ often feel powerless and out of control. Furthermore, it's often hard to see this power in others. Unlike the members of the early Church, many modern-day Catholics completely adapt to secular culture. There seems to be nothing different about them. They may pray occasionally and attend Mass on Sunday, but they often act as if they were atheists. How is this possible, given the internal presence of the Holy Spirit?

The answer is simple. Just because we are temples of the Holy Spirit doesn't automatically mean that the Spirit is active and visible in our lives. We have some responsibility in the process too.

Let's look at an example that will help illustrate this point. Suppose my wife gives me a new sweater for Christmas. It is folded neatly in a cardboard box, wrapped with red paper, and adorned with a shiny green bow. To use my gift, I must first unwrap the box, take out the sweater, and put it on. But, if I choose, I can put the unopened gift in a closet and leave it there for months or years. That doesn't mean that I never received the gift; it simply means that I'm not using it.

The same concept applies to the Holy Spirit. Having the "power" means nothing unless I make a conscious decision to open the box and use it.

IS THE SPIRIT WORKING IN YOUR LIFE?

So, how do you know if the Holy Spirit is working in your life? Is it a matter of speaking in tongues and performing miracles? Not necessarily. If you are being led by the Holy Spirit, your life will produce good fruit. That fruit is represented by your thoughts, words, and deeds.

As detailed by St. Paul in his letter to the Galatians, a life guided by the Spirit will produce the following fruit: *love, joy, peace, patience, kindness, goodness, faithfulness, gentleness, and self-control* (5:22–23, RSVCE). We will look at each of these fruits in detail in the second part of this book, but let's take a moment and read through that list again. Can you imagine being consistently loving, joyful, peaceful, patient, kind, good, faithful, gentle, and in control of your passions?

Maybe you're thinking, *That sounds like a description of Jesus, not of me!* In all honesty, most of us would be happy if our lives were producing one or two of these fruits on a regular basis. Am I right? Unfortunately, thinking like that underestimates the dynamic power of the Holy Spirit. Yes, all of those fruits were present in the life of Christ, but they can be evident in our lives as well. It is possible for each of us to be transformed so that we consistently produce good fruit.

ABIDE . . . AND THRIVE

Speaking to his disciples, Jesus said, "It was not you who chose me, but I who chose you and appointed you to go and bear fruit that will remain" (Jn 15:16). Although we are imperfect sinners, Jesus calls each of us by name and commissions us to bear fruit that will last.

Once again, he would not expect us to do something that is impossible. There are two possible reasons we don't see this good fruit in our lives: Either we assume that it's an unattainable goal, or we try to get there on our own. No matter how hard we try, we will never consistently bear good fruit on our own. Jesus said it best: "Remain in me, as I remain in you. Just as a branch cannot bear fruit on its own unless it remains on the vine, so neither can you unless you remain in me. I am the vine, you are the branches. Whoever remains in me and I in him will bear much fruit, because without me you can do nothing" (Jn 15:4–5).

If we want to bear abundant, good fruit we must remain connected to Jesus, letting him work through us. St. Paul showed his grasp of this concept when he wrote in Galatians 2:20, "I live, no longer I, but Christ lives in me." As I mentioned earlier, the Spirit of Jesus comes to live in us at Baptism and is strengthened through the sacrament of Confirmation. Because of this amazing gift, we have what we need to produce Christlike fruit in our lives!

Don't get me wrong—living this kind of life can be challenging. Even with the Holy Spirit dwelling in us and the help of prayer and the sacraments, producing good fruit is not automatic. Because of our fallen human nature, there exists a tension between the desires of the flesh (the things of the world) and the desires of the Spirit. Quite frankly, there are times when I know what God wants me to do, but I choose to do what I want instead. St. Paul addressed this ongoing struggle in his letter to the Galatians: "I say, then: live by the Spirit and you will certainly not gratify the desire of the flesh. For the flesh has desires against the Spirit, and the Spirit against the flesh; these are opposed to each other, so that you may not do what you want" (5:16–17).

WHY FIGHT IT?

Even though we may struggle, this is a battle we *must* fight. Our salvation depends on it. Though we often make excuses and downplay our sinfulness, Jesus clearly states what will happen if our lives don't bear good fruit: "Just so, every good tree bears good fruit, and a rotten tree bears bad fruit. A good tree cannot bear bad fruit, nor can a rotten tree bear good fruit. *Every tree that does not bear good fruit will be cut down and thrown into the fire.* So by their fruits you will know them" (Mt 7:17–20, emphasis mine).

Wow! At the end of our lives, we will be judged by the fruit that we produced. Think about that for a minute. No good fruit means no heaven. It's a tough message, but one that we need to hear. Before we start worrying about the possibility of spending eternity in hell, however, let's recall what we discussed earlier: *Jesus does not expect us to do the impossible.*

With the help of the Holy Spirit, bearing good fruit is a realistic goal. Letting the Spirit work in us will not only enable us to bear good fruit and give us the peace that we seek but also allow us to spend eternity in heaven.

Believe it or not, you are already on your way to living the life that God has planned for you. The fact that you are reading this book implies that you aren't satisfied with a life rooted solely in materialism and earthly comfort. You are seeking something more, and the Lord will not let you down. By setting your mind on "what is above, not . . . what is on earth" (Col 3:2), you are traveling on the road that will allow you to "have life and have it more abundantly" (Jn 10:10). According to St. Paul:

> Those who live according to the flesh are concerned with the things of the flesh, but those who live according to the spirit with the things of the spirit. The concern of the flesh is death, but the concern of the spirit is life and peace. For the concern of the flesh is hostility toward God; it does not submit to the law of God, nor can it;

and those who are in the flesh cannot please God.
(Rom 8:5–8)

I want you to once more envision your life filled with love, joy, peace, patience, kindness, goodness, faithfulness, gentleness, and self-control. Sounds exciting, doesn't it? It is a very realistic goal, which begins with setting your mind on the things of the Spirit, giving him permission to work in your life, and frequently repeating that powerful three-word prayer: "Come, Holy Spirit!"

REMEMBER

1. Through the sacraments of Baptism and Confirmation we receive the full power of the Holy Spirit.

2. Our lives cannot bear good fruit without the help of the Holy Spirit.

3. The fruit of the Spirit is love, joy, peace, patience, kindness, goodness, faithfulness, gentleness, and self-control (Gal 5:22–23).

4. At the end of our life, we will be judged by our fruit.

5. We must give the Holy Spirit permission to work in our lives.

REFLECT

1. Do you feel the power of the Holy Spirit in your life? List some specific examples.

2. If you asked a friend to describe you, would your friend use words such as *loving, joyful, peaceful, patient, kind, good, faithful, gentle*, and *self-controlled*?

3. Which of the fruits of the Holy Spirit is most lacking in your life?

4. Do you ever pray for the grace to bear good fruit, or do you try to accomplish good things through willpower and perseverance alone?

5. Is anything holding you back from surrendering to the Holy Spirit and letting him work in your life? If so, are you willing to at least ask for the *desire* to surrender to him?

RESPOND

Think about the power that you already possess in the Holy Spirit. Make the decision that you will do whatever is necessary to activate that power in your life.

LET'S PRAY

Dear Holy Spirit, I know that I don't have what it takes to be holy, but that's okay. Jesus promised that you will give me the power that I lack. I want that power, and I pray for the grace to yield control of my life to you. In Jesus' name I pray. Amen.

2

Will This Work for Me?

Why spend your money for what is not bread; your
wages for what does not satisfy?
—Isaiah 55:2

I hope that you are already beginning to see that it is possible for you to live a peaceful, Spirit-led life and produce an abundance of good fruit. The fact that the world is crazy doesn't take away that possibility, nor does the fact that your own life is filled with problems and challenges. What if you have a lukewarm faith, love comfort, or consider yourself a world-class worrier? And what if you have embarked on a never-ending quest for happiness that always seems to elude you? No problem! I guarantee that what you read in this book can transform your life and give you the peace you desire. How can I be so sure? Let me tell you my story, and I think you'll understand.

Most of my life has been devoted to the pursuit of happiness and comfort, with no real awareness of God's presence. Until my surrender to the Holy Spirit, my goal was just to make it through the day at school or work, go home, and find a way to escape from reality. On the surface I seemed reasonably happy, but inside I was miserable. You may be able to relate to some of the details I share in this chapter. That wouldn't surprise me at all. The world is filled with people who are trying to find happiness, but looking in the wrong places.

MY STORY

I was born and raised in northeast Philadelphia and lived a typical middle-class life. I have one sister who is seven years younger than me. My family attended Mass every Sunday, and my sister and I went to Catholic school. I knew that I was loved, and all of my needs were met. There was no reason for me to be anxious, but I was. From the time I was in the first grade, I worried that my parents might die or that I would get beaten up in school. My greatest source of anxiety, however, was the fear of having a serious disease.

I was an anxious mess, but it never occurred to me to ask God for help with my daily struggles. For some reason, he just didn't seem real to me. Thinking back on it, I can understand why. God was never mentioned outside of church or school, and I never heard anyone speak of him as a real person who could help with life's ordinary problems. As a result, the first eighteen years of my life were filled with anxiety and hopelessness.

My college years brought a temporary decrease in my health concerns, mainly because they were replaced with a fear of flunking out (this one was actually grounded in reality, as I came frighteningly close) and anxiety about finding a job after graduation. During this period, I also struggled with low self-esteem and loneliness. My one serious romantic relationship ended abruptly (I got dumped!), and I didn't handle it well at all. To say I felt hopeless would be putting it mildly. As he often does when we hit rock bottom, however, the Lord was about to make himself known in a big way.

At about that time, my parish was assigned a priest who changed my life. Fr. Dave Jakubiec was a Franciscan who helped out with the weekend Masses. He was warm, funny, and engaging. His homilies brought the Bible to life for me, and he constantly emphasized the importance of having a personal relationship with Jesus Christ. Fr. Dave stressed that the Lord wants to be involved in our daily lives and can help us with our problems. For the first time, I felt that Jesus was real and believed that he could actually help me!

Fr. Dave also led a Catholic Charismatic Renewal prayer group at a nearby parish. My best friend Ray eventually started to attend these prayer meetings and tried to persuade me to come to just one meeting. I knew virtually nothing about the Charismatic Renewal and it sounded weird to me, so initially I resisted. Ray was persistent, however, and I finally gave in.

As soon as we walked in the door, I knew that this was going to be something extraordinary. I noticed that almost everyone was carrying a Bible and speaking openly about Jesus. I had never experienced anything like this before. As the evening progressed, I witnessed several hundred people praying in tongues, prophesying, reading scripture, and loudly praising the Lord. At first I had to fight the urge to run out the door, but the group eventually began to pique my interest. These Catholics were so filled with joy, and they talked about

Jesus as if they really knew him. When they prayed for miracles, it was apparent that they believed their prayers would be heard and answered. I was still put off by the weirdness factor, but they had something that I wanted.

I decided to return the following week . . . and then the week after that. Before long, I was a regular. Ray and I attended the prayer meeting regularly for a year. It took a while for me to pray with my arms outstretched, but it eventually did happen. I was baptized in the Holy Spirit (more on that later) and received the gift of tongues. In that prayer group, Jesus became real to me.

My life outside these meetings began to change, too. Ray and I sometimes had impromptu prayer meetings in his car, praising the Lord and asking for his assistance with our daily challenges. Fr. Dave agreed to open up the friary chapel for us on Friday evenings so that we could adore Jesus in the Blessed Sacrament. I began to feel the peace and hope I so desperately wanted.

I'm not sure why, but after a while Ray and I stopped going to the prayer meetings and I gradually resumed my old ways. All was not lost, however. Although I didn't realize it at the time, the Lord had planted seeds that would continue to bear fruit years later.

WORRY WARS

I graduated from college in the midst of a serious recession and had a difficult time finding a job. My search for employment was further hindered by lack of direction and a low GPA. After four months of worrying and job hunting, I settled for a low-paying job with the federal government, doing something I didn't want to do. My hypochondria returned with a vengeance, and I began to experience heart palpitations and panic attacks. On several occasions family members took me to the emergency room. I felt light-headed and my heart was racing, so I was sure I was having a heart attack. The fact that all diagnostic tests came back negative didn't stop me from believing that the doctors had missed something. I truly believed that I wouldn't live to see the age of thirty.

I had to do something. Stress, anxiety, and hopelessness were taking a toll on my career and my personal life. The thought of having a panic attack made me think twice about going out in public. While at the office, I often had to take breaks and walk around the parking lot to compose myself. It was time for me to seek help.

Now, I'd like to tell you that I ran into the open arms of Jesus and sought the rest (Mt 11:28) and peace (Jn 20:19) that he promises. But that's not exactly the approach I took. Ignoring what I had learned during twelve years of Catholic school, my experience with the charismatic prayer meetings, and weekly Mass attendance, I came up with a "better" plan. I decided that the best way to cure my anxiety was through alcohol, shopping, and self-indulgence in cigarettes, fast food, and various forms of mindless entertainment. I was determined to find peace, and to a certain extent, this plan did bring me relief. When I was out drinking and chain-smoking with my friends, my fears seemed to fade away. They would return in the morning (along with a nasty hangover), which drove me to repeat the "medication" in the evening.

I also discovered the therapeutic effect of buying "toys" for myself. Purchasing CDs, DVDs, vintage comic books, baseball cards, books, and other memorabilia made me feel good. To maintain the good mood, however, I had to buy more and more "stuff." I didn't give it much thought at the time, but there were many problems with my lifestyle. I was totally self-centered, routinely falling into serious sin, and, although I never missed Mass, had no real relationship with God.

By the time I turned thirty, I was very unhappy with my life. I wasn't making enough money to move out of my parents' house, and I felt like a failure. Even though I lacked marketable experience, I knew I somehow had to find a better-paying job. It would take a miracle to command the salary necessary to live on my own, but I had to try. I updated my résumé and applied for several positions. It was now a matter of waiting for a lucky break . . . or a miracle.

A MIRACULOUS NOVENA

A week after I sent in the job applications, a visiting priest announced that he would lead a Miraculous Medal novena after Mass. I didn't know what that involved and wasn't looking for any extra church activities, but something Father said resonated with me: many miracles have resulted from this novena. "When we ask for Mary's intercession, she immediately presents our needs to Jesus," he explained.

Filled with hope and in need of a miracle, I waited around after Mass to attend the first night of the novena and asked the Blessed Mother to help me find a new job. Believing that

I was on to something big, I decided to return to church each evening for the remainder of the novena.

A few nights later, I arrived home from the bar (my post-novena destination) to find a message on my answering machine. One of the companies I applied to was interested in setting up an interview. A week later, I was offered the job and a 50 percent salary increase! I thanked the Blessed Mother profusely . . . but the excitement wore off in a few days and I went back to my old ways. Because of the salary increase, I finally moved out and purchased my own home. Unfortunately, I spent much of the extra money on beer, "toys," and entertainment. Once again, I was in a rut and feeling miserable.

I had moved to New Jersey and joined a new parish. One Sunday at Mass, the priest announced the formation of a new social/spiritual group for those in their twenties and thirties. The meetings would be structured around the Rosary, Benediction, teaching, and social activities. While my primary motivation was to meet a nice Catholic girl, there was something slightly attractive about the spiritual dimension of the group and I decided to attend the first meeting. Praying the Rosary brought me some comfort, Benediction was fine (as a former altar server, I was familiar with it), and the guest speaker gave an inspiring talk. Best of all, the people seemed somewhat normal.

I decided to keep attending, though it had very little to do with my own spiritual growth. Once I met a young woman to date, I told myself, I would quit the group to avoid turning into a religious fanatic. I liked being Catholic, but Mass on Sunday was enough of a commitment for me!

A CHANGE OF HEART

While I was waiting for my future wife to turn up, I became more and more involved in the group, writing and printing the newsletter, providing the worship music, and helping with anything else that was needed. For the first time, I was serving the Lord (and other people) instead of myself, and it felt good. I made some great friends, and I was no longer concerned about being a religious fanatic. My new life was bringing me peace, and I liked that.

Soon I met a beautiful young lady named Eileen and knew that she was "the one." Things clicked; we started dating, got engaged, and were married the following year. To find someone as wonderful as Eileen was absolutely miraculous, and I was grateful that the Lord had sent her into my life. We continued to be members of the group until it disbanded a few months later. My life was finally on the right track.

At this point, I made the mistake of thinking that the rest of my life would be problem free. Within the first five years of our marriage, however, as Eileen and I started our family, we experienced many difficult moments, including infertility and high-risk pregnancy, our daughters' premature births, and one daughter's diagnosis with autism.

You would think that by now there was no way I could go back to my lukewarm, fear-filled way of life. Guess again. Although I still attended Mass each week, I barely prayed and was worrying constantly. What little free time I could carve out was spent in front of the TV or computer. While it's true that I wasn't producing as much bad fruit, I wasn't producing much good fruit either. Once again, the stage was set for the Lord to intervene in my life in a *big* way.

A MEDICAL SCARE

I started to experience unusual physical symptoms: nausea, abdominal pain, weight loss, and dizziness when lying down. My wife finally persuaded me to go to the doctor, and the diagnostic tests showed that the lymph nodes in my abdomen were enlarged. The doctors suspected that I was suffering from lymphoma, and my life was suddenly turned upside down. I launched into full-blown panic mode, believing that I'd soon be meeting the Lord in judgment. I had to get ready!

Practically overnight, I started praying, reading the Bible, listening to Catholic radio, and attending daily Mass. As the weeks passed, an unexpected peace came over me. Sure, the medical testing was ongoing, and the possibility of cancer was looking more likely, but I was experiencing the "peace of God that surpasses all understanding" (Phil 4:7) and it blew me away. Nothing else mattered to me except remaining close to Jesus, and I surrendered my life to him.

Six months later my symptoms disappeared, and my lymph nodes returned to their normal size. The doctors couldn't explain it, but I could. Just like the apostles, I had encountered Jesus Christ in the midst of the storm, and he saved me. And this time, I told myself, *there would be no turning back.*

As you read my story, did you notice how the Lord was constantly reaching out to me through people and circumstances?

He was not deterred by the fact that I wasn't listening at times. He kept after me, and I'm glad he did. Conversion is an ongoing process, and it unfolds gradually in our lives. Like the Israelites, we sometimes veer off course and turn away from God and toward idols of our own making (in my case, the idol of pleasure!). And yet the Lord remains faithful to each of us. When we turn back to him, and yield to the power of the Holy Spirit, our lives once again bear good fruit. Following our own desires, on the other hand, produces only rotten fruit and misery.

Don't be discouraged if you feel lukewarm, weak, and incapable of being led by the Holy Spirit. You don't have to remain stuck in a rut. If I can do it, so can you! In the next chapter, we will discuss how you too can give your life to Jesus and stir up the power of the Holy Spirit. Take it from me: it's the best decision you'll ever make.

REMEMBER

1. Our desire for happiness is actually a longing for God.

2. "Draw near to God, and he will draw near to you" (Jas 4:8).

3. Trying to find happiness by indulging in the pleasures of the world does not work.

4. The Lord is constantly pursuing us, even when we are not paying attention.

5. Conversion is an ongoing process and unfolds gradually in our lives.

REFLECT

1. Is Jesus real to you? Do you turn to him with your problems?

2. Do you speak to your heavenly Father? How about the Holy Spirit?

3. Have you ever sought happiness in the things of the world? How did it work out?

4. Do you ever feel that the Holy Spirit is calling you to do something? How do you typically respond?

5. Has anyone in your life introduced you to Jesus? If so, have you thanked them?

RESPOND

Ask the Holy Spirit to open your eyes so you can see the areas in your life that need improvement. Then turn to Jesus and tell him you're ready to be transformed.

LET'S PRAY

Dear Jesus, I know that I have ignored you many times in the past, but I want to change. I have tried it my way, and it hasn't worked. This time is different. I want to know you and follow your lead. I want to yield control to your Spirit. I may be weak, but I believe it is possible. Please grant me the grace to keep my eyes on you and continue moving forward. In your mighty name I pray. Amen.

3

Activating the Power of the Spirit

> While meeting with them, he enjoined them not to depart from Jerusalem, but to wait for the "promise of the Father about which you have heard me speak; for John baptized with water, but in a few days you will be baptized with the holy Spirit."
> —Acts 1:4–5

My walk with the Lord has hardly been a direct route. Like the Israelites who took forty years to make an eleven-day journey to the Promised Land (Dt 1:2), at times I have been stubborn, making the trip more complicated than it had to be. It's as if the Lord was standing on the street in front of me with outstretched arms, but I spent decades going around the block, taking numerous detours and even traveling to other cities before I ran into his embrace.

Despite my stumbling, I have arrived at the point where Jesus is a close friend, and we are walking through life together. Although our relationship continues to grow (as it should), I would say that I'm in a good place right now. I am much more willing to trust him than I was five years ago. And while I can't say that I never experience moments of doubt or anxiety, my life is filled with peace. External circumstances don't bother me as they once did. As long as I have the Father, Son, and Holy Spirit in my life, all is well.

Simply telling you about *my* life, however, won't give you the peace that *you* seek, nor will it help you grow closer to the Lord. I need to give you something concrete that you can apply in your own life.

Because my relationship with Jesus has developed gradually, over the span of many years, it's tough for me to pinpoint one event that made the difference. However, as I pondered my spiritual journey (while writing this book), it occurred to me that there was indeed one specific experience that changed everything. My life before and after this experience looked radically different. That life-changing event was baptism in the Holy Spirit.

BAPTISM IN THE HOLY SPIRIT

What exactly is baptism in the Holy Spirit? Essentially, it is a stirring up of the graces we receive in the sacraments of Baptism and Confirmation. While not a sacrament itself, it has been known to produce dramatic results. Those who are baptized in the Holy Spirit generally experience a strong sense of the Father's love ("Father, I know in my heart that you love me"), a desire to submit to the Lordship of Christ ("Jesus, I want you to rule over all areas of my life"), and a willingness to be led by the Holy Spirit ("Come, Holy Spirit. Let me know what I should do"). Some (but not all) who are baptized in the Spirit also receive the gift of prayer tongues, prophecy, or healing.

If it's so great, you may wonder, why is it that so few people seem to know about it? I don't know the answer to that, but I do believe that baptism in the Holy Spirit may be the best-kept secret in the Catholic Church. With the exception of those involved in the Catholic Charismatic Renewal, the vast majority of Catholics have never heard of it. But, before you assume that it's some sort of top-secret ritual reserved for a handful of individuals, check out the following comment from Pope Francis. Speaking to fifty thousand people gathered at the Catholic Charismatic Renewal Convention in 2014, the Holy Father said, "I expect from you that you share with everyone in the Church the grace of baptism in the Holy Spirit (an expression we find in the Acts of the Apostles)."[1]

Did you catch that? Pope Francis is imploring those familiar with baptism in the Holy Spirit to share their knowledge with everyone in the Church! The fact that it's still relatively unknown shows that there is much work to be done. Surprisingly, Francis isn't the first pope to promote baptism in the Holy Spirit to the entire Church. In a 2008 Pentecost address, Pope Benedict XVI expressed his desire for everyone to discover the power of baptism in the Holy Spirit: "Today I would like to extend the invitation to all: Let us rediscover, dear brothers and sisters, the beauty of being baptized in the Holy Spirit; let us recover awareness of our Baptism and our Confirmation, ever timely sources of grace. Let us ask the Virgin Mary to obtain also today a renewed Pentecost for the

Church that will imbue in all, and especially in the young, the joy of living and witnessing to the Gospel" (*Regina Caeli*, May 11, 2008).

Note that Pope Benedict refers to the grace available through the sacraments of Baptism and Confirmation, but he does not state that those sacraments will bear fruit automatically. As we discussed earlier, the fact that we receive the Holy Spirit in Baptism doesn't guarantee that our lives will bear good fruit. At some point, we must make a conscious decision to follow Christ and give the Spirit permission to act.

Pope St. John Paul II addressed this point in his 1979 apostolic exhortation, *Catechesi Tradendae* (*On Catechesis in Our Time*), when he emphasized that the sacrament of Baptism only gives us the *capacity* to believe. To enter into a deep, personal relationship with Jesus and bear lasting fruit, we need something else: "A certain number of children baptized in infancy come for catechesis in the parish without receiving any other initiation into the faith and still without any explicit personal attachment to Jesus Christ; they only have the capacity to believe placed within them by Baptism and the presence of the Holy Spirit."

Baptism in the Holy Spirit is offered at many Catholic parishes around the world and administered as part of Life in the Spirit seminars. Having people pray over you as you surrender to the Spirit can be a powerful spiritual experience.[2] To learn more about baptism in the Holy Spirit and the Catholic Charismatic Renewal, check out the following books:

- *Breath of God: Living a Life Led by the Holy Spirit* (Fr. Dave Pivonka, Ave Maria Press, 2015)

- *Baptism in the Holy Spirit* (International Catholic Charismatic Renewal Services Doctrinal Commission, 2017)

- *A Mighty Current of Grace: The Story of the Catholic Charismatic Renewal* (Alan Schreck, The Word Among Us Press, 2017)

Of course, you don't need to attend a seminar or be prayed over publicly in a prayer meeting to receive this spiritual gift. In fact, it is surprisingly simple to unleash the power of the Holy Spirit in your life. It can be experienced privately and casually, while sitting in your living room. What matters most is not the method you choose but having a sincere desire to allow the Holy Spirit to work in your life.

Some time ago I had the privilege of interviewing David Mangan on my morning radio show (*Spirit in the Morning* on Holy Spirit Radio in Philadelphia). In February 1967, he participated in the weekend retreat at Duquesne University that is generally recognized as the beginning of the Catholic Charismatic Renewal. During the interview, he spoke of being at that retreat and having a desire for the power of the Holy Spirit (the "dynamite" we talked about earlier). Entering the adoration chapel, he was suddenly filled with an overwhelming feeling of God's presence and love, followed by the experience of praying in tongues. Asking for the "dynamite" was all it took!

When I questioned David about the best way to receive this powerful outpouring of the Holy Spirit, his answer was simple and to the point. "Ask for it," he told me, "and then thank God because you know he just answered your prayer."

"Even if you don't feel anything?" I questioned.

He immediately responded, "Even if you don't feel anything!"

While it seems a bit bold, his answer is actually grounded in scripture. Speaking about our heavenly Father's desire to give us good things, Jesus had this to say:

> And I tell you, ask and you will receive; seek and you will find; knock and the door will be opened to you. For everyone who asks, receives; and the one who seeks, finds; and to the one who knocks, the door will be opened. What father among you would hand his son a snake when he asks for a fish? Or hand him a scorpion when he asks for an egg? If you then, who are wicked, know how to give good gifts to your children, how much more will the Father in heaven give the holy Spirit to those who ask him? (Lk 11:9–13)

If we ask our Father for a new outpouring of the Holy Spirit, our request will be granted. Period! That's why we can thank him even if we don't feel a thing. Jesus' own words assure us that our heavenly Father will not deny this request.

With that in mind, how should we ask? It can be as simple as saying, "Father, fill me with your Holy Spirit," or "Father, baptize me in your Holy Spirit." That's all there is to it! At the end of this chapter, you will have the chance to pray this prayer, and I strongly encourage you to do so. Even if you decide to pursue baptism in the Holy Spirit with a charismatic prayer group, I urge you to pray the prayer now. It will begin to bear fruit as soon as you utter the words.

HARVESTTIME

Now that you've read my story, you may be wondering why it took so long for baptism in the Holy Spirit to yield any significant good fruit in my life. After all, it happened while I was in college. Why the big delay?

That's a really good question. Here's the answer in a nutshell: *The work of producing good fruit is a joint effort between you and the Holy Spirit.* The first step is to invite the Spirit to work in your life (in my case, through baptism in the Holy Spirit). Giving him permission to act, however, is only the beginning. After doing that, you must then be open to his prompting. For me, that has been an on-again, off-again process.

In the second part of this book, we will explore each of the fruits of the Spirit mentioned in Paul's letter to the Galatians (5:22–23). As we discuss the various fruits, we must bear in mind two important principles:

1. Each of these fruits can be expressed in many different ways in the Christian life; and

2. When the Holy Spirit prompts us to exercise these virtues, we have the ability to ignore his suggestions.

In my case, after initially giving the Holy Spirit the go-ahead to work in my life, I became distracted by the pleasures of the world and tuned him out for many years. Like your car's GPS, the Holy Spirit will not force you to listen to him!

Additionally, asking to be filled with the Holy Spirit should not be something we do only once. We need to ask again and again, each time we see those fruits diminish (or weeds like anger and stress sprouting back out). When asked why he had received so many infillings of the Holy Spirit, evangelist Dwight L. Moody reportedly replied, "I leak"![3] That pretty much sums it up for all of us. We have a tendency to leak. Therefore, we should keep asking the Father to fill us up.

Again, there is a scriptural basis for this practice. The Bible states that the Holy Spirit descended on the apostles at Pentecost and they were "filled with the holy Spirit" (Acts 2:4), but that doesn't mean they never had to ask again. Later, after being released from captivity, Peter and John prayed for the grace to speak God's word with boldness (Acts 4:29), and guess what happened? "As they prayed, the place where they were gathered shook, and they were all filled with the holy Spirit and continued to speak the word of God with boldness" (Acts 4:31).

In response to their prayer, they were once more filled with the Holy Spirit. Praying for a new outpouring of the Holy Spirit is critical when spreading the word of God in a hostile environment (as in Peter and John's case), but it's also important before making decisions, going to work, or interacting with family and friends. We should ask for this outpouring of the Spirit throughout the day, confident that our prayer will be answered.

Before moving on to discuss what our lives can look like if we follow the Spirit, I want to make an important point. It is not necessary to be part of the Catholic Charismatic Renewal to be led by the Holy Spirit. Doing so helped me tremendously and I believe it can help you, but the Holy Spirit belongs to the whole Church, not to any one particular group. He is standing by, ready to step into action. You just have to say the word and follow his lead!

REMEMBER

1.   Baptism in the Holy Spirit is a stirring up of the graces received in the sacraments of Baptism and Confirmation.

2.   The main effects of baptism in the Holy Spirit are a strong sense of God's love, a desire to submit to the Lordship of Christ, and a willingness to follow the Holy Spirit.

3.   Baptism in the Holy Spirit can be received in a communal setting or in your own home.

4.   When we ask the Father for a new outpouring of the Holy Spirit, we will not be denied.

5.   We should ask for this outpouring often, even several times each day.

REFLECT

1.   Ask the Father to send the Holy Spirit to you. Did you feel anything? If not, do you believe Jesus' words that your request was granted?

2.   Do you have any fears about surrendering your life to the Spirit? What are they?

3.   Do you know anyone that you believe is led by the Holy Spirit? How can you tell?

4.   Think back over the past day. How many times have you sought the help of the Holy Spirit?

5.   Do you find evangelization and living a Christian life difficult? If so, why? What can you do to make it easier?

RESPOND

Ask God to fill you with the Holy Spirit, and expect something to happen.

LET'S PRAY

Heavenly Father, Jesus assures us that you will not deny those who request a fresh outpouring of the Holy Spirit. With that in mind, I ask you to baptize me in your Holy Spirit. Thank you for saying yes! I welcome you, Holy Spirit. I want to be transformed into the image of Christ. Open my heart so that I'm willing to follow your lead. In Jesus' name I pray. Amen.

Part II

The Fruits of the Holy Spirit

4

Love

This I command you: love one another.
—John 15:17

Although love is the most important fruit of the Holy Spirit, it's also the least understood. If you put the word "love" in an internet search engine, the results will probably include the words "feeling," "desire," or "romance." According to advertisers, we express love for others by buying expensive gifts. According to the media, celebrity couples fall in and out of love every day. We speak of loving everything from sports to chocolate cake.

In Matthew 22:36–39, Jesus tells us that the greatest commandment is to love God and the second greatest is to love our neighbor. This brings us to an important question—what exactly is love?

According to St. Thomas Aquinas, "To love is to will the good of another."[4] Contrary to what the world believes, love is not a feeling. While it is true that affection often accompanies love, that isn't always the case—particularly when we are overwhelmed with other strong feelings, such as stress or anger. At those times, we can choose to love by making a conscious decision, without feeling anything. It is possible to grit your teeth and force yourself to love those who drive you crazy. But, as we will discuss shortly, we shouldn't settle for loving in this way. For now, however, just remember that love is not a feeling. It is a decision.

To better understand the love referred to by St. Paul in his list of fruits, we should recall that his original manuscript was written in Greek. In the English language, we use the word "love" in a wide variety of situations. For example, I can love my dog, football, pizza, or my spouse. And, while we understand that the love in each of those expressions is different, we use the same word. In Greek, however, there are multiple words for love. (If you want to find out more about this, check out Pope Benedict XVI's general audience of May 24, 2006, on the Vatican website, where he describes the difference between *phileo*, or friendship, and *agape*, or self-sacrificial love.)

"Agape," which refers to the highest form of love, is the word St. Paul uses in his list of fruits of the Holy Spirit. Jesus used the same word in describing the Father's love for him and his love for us (Jn 15:9). It is an extremely powerful word.

LEARNING TO LOVE LIKE JESUS

Let's unpack one of the most challenging passages in the entire Bible. These two verses sum up what it means to be a Christian: "This is my commandment: love one another as I love you. No one has greater love than this, to lay down one's life for one's friends" (Jn 15:12–13).

Jesus uses the word "love" three times in this passage. Can you guess what Greek word appears in the original manuscript? I'll give you a hint. He uses the same word each time. Yep. When the Lord commands us to love one another, when he speaks of the love he has for us, and when he describes the greatest act of love, he uses the word "agape."

Take note that this isn't just a suggestion. It's a commandment. Jesus commands us to love others with the same self-sacrificial love that he has for us. And you don't need me to tell you that he gave up his life for us. Jesus means business! He said what he meant, and he meant what he said.

Does the thought of loving like that—to the point of willingly giving up your life for someone else—shake you up a little? *Wait a minute,* you might say. *Loving like that sounds humanly impossible.* I totally agree. Loving like that *is* humanly impossible. That's why Jesus sent the Holy Spirit to fill our hearts with divine love! "God's love has been poured into our hearts through the Holy Spirit who has been given to us" (Rom 5:5).

With the help of the Holy Spirit, you have the power to love with a pure, self-sacrificial love. And I'm not just talking about loving those who are nice to you. With the Spirit's help, it's possible for you to love even your enemies with an agape love. Remember our discussion about giving the Holy Spirit permission to work in your life? If you let yourself become docile to the Spirit, you can put this type of love into practice. Even though it seems unimaginable, you have within you all you need to love your enemies with a pure and self-sacrificial love.

A personal example comes to mind. Earlier, I touched on the story of getting dumped by my girlfriend in college. It was a very traumatic experience for me. As she delivered the news, she rattled off many reasons for the breakup. Apparently, I had been on "probation" for a long time and didn't realize it. By the time she told me, my window for improving had already closed. Her mind was made up.

Once I got past the shock and hurt, I was overcome by anger. To make matters worse, I soon discovered that she was dating a friend of mine (and a fellow member of the parish music ministry!). I fully expected her to come to her senses and come back to me, but it never happened. Several months later, they became engaged. Now, because we were all members of the same music ministry, I was invited to the wedding. I was still hurt and angry, but I felt (Holy Spirit?) that I should go. I drove to the wedding with my friend Ray and his girlfriend. Believe it or not, I was filled with peace during the ceremony. I guarantee that this peace did not come from me. That was the Holy Spirit in action!

The same Spirit who allowed Jesus to give up his life for those he loved comes to live in us when we are baptized. We receive not a cheap imitation or a partial version but the one and only Holy Spirit who guided the Lord. Why, then, is it so easy for us to post nasty comments on social media, engage in gossip, use foul language, and scream at family members and coworkers? Jesus didn't behave like that. He may have spoken firmly at times, but everything he said and did was motivated by love. Why is it different for us? The Holy Spirit waits for permission to act in our lives. It's up to us to invite him to move in our lives. When we pray "Come, Holy Spirit," we stir up the Spirit of Jesus and let him go to work.

HOLY SPIRIT, LEAD US TO LOVE

How about if you're praying "Come, Holy Spirit" and still manage to fly off the handle on a regular basis? My initial recommendation would be to ask more frequently. It takes two seconds to pray, "Come, Holy Spirit," and there are 86,400 seconds in a day. Subtracting 28,800 seconds (eight hours) for sleep leaves us with 57,600 seconds. That gives us the opportunity for 28,800 "Come, Holy Spirits" per day! Now, that's not practical or even possible for most of us, but we can build up those invitations gradually, especially in moments when we feel agitated, irritated, or angry. As we reach out for divine help, each of those temptations becomes an occasion of grace. How? Each time we invite the Holy Spirit to come alive, he responds.

In addition to using this prayer when you are troubled, it's a good idea to get into the habit of praying this prayer at regular intervals: when you wake up, on the way to the office, before responding to emails, when you're about to deal with someone who "pushes your buttons." Every minute of every day provides a new opportunity to invoke the Holy Spirit. Do it!

Inviting the Holy Spirit to come alive is incredibly effective and important, but it's still not enough. We must also respond to his promptings. Because of free will, the final decision to obey the Holy Spirit rests with us. When we ask for his help, he will advise us (mainly through thoughts or feelings) to refrain from posting that offensive comment on Facebook or telling our coworker what we really think, but he won't force us to love someone. He will certainly make it easier, but he won't compel us to act against our will.

Sooner or later, we all have to deal with someone who just seems unlovable. It may be the loud neighbor with body odor, the know-it-all at the office, the "holier-than-thou" person at daily Mass, or even a close friend or relative who seems perpetually embroiled in some personal drama (often of their own making). We all know at least one person like that. Let's call him Joe Annoying. I can force myself to obey Jesus and follow the prompting of the Holy Spirit, but that will only get me so far. Eventually, I'm bound to have a bad day and refuse to love Joe. Before I know it, I'm yelling at Joe or secretly hoping that something bad happens to him. I might be so annoyed that I remove him from my prayer list or just happen to "forget" about praying for him. This happens when our hearts become hardened.

Our fallen human nature makes us tend to be selfish and uncaring. It sometimes feels like we can't control our actions. Even though we know what we should do, we end up doing the opposite. "I know that Jesus wants me to love Joe, but I don't feel like it. I just don't have it in me today. He's too annoying!" St. Paul describes this dilemma in his letter to the Romans:

> What I do, I do not understand. For I do not do what I want, but I do what I hate. Now if I do what I do not want, I concur that the law is good. So now it is no longer I who do it, but sin

that dwells in me. For I know that good does not
dwell in me, that is, in my flesh. The willing is
ready at hand, but doing the good is not. For I
do not do the good I want, but I do the evil I do
not want. Now if I do what I do not want, it is
no longer I who do it, but sin that dwells in me.
(Rom 7:15–20)

LOVING THE UNLOVABLE

Fortunately, there is something we can do about this. In addition to praying and following the prompting of the Holy Spirit, we can bear certain things in mind as we try to love the Joe Annoyings out there. It requires work, but it's worth it. Focusing on the following truths will make it easier to overcome your feelings and love Joe with an agape love, even when you'd rather slap him!

- *We are all children of God.* Joe Annoying is God's precious child. The Lord loves him with an unconditional love and sent his Son to die on the Cross for him. God designed and created Joe because the universe wasn't complete without him. Refusing to love Joe deeply grieves the Lord.

- *Joe Annoying is created in God's image and likeness.* No matter how hard it can be to fathom, every human being is created in the image and likeness of God. The terrorist, the serial killer, the child molester, even Joe Annoying! You may have to fall back on your intellect on this one. Even if you don't feel it, keep reminding yourself of this important fact. Failing to grasp this truth can lead to hardness of heart, bitterness, and hatred.

- *Joe Annoying has good qualities.* This one is particularly important for the Joes we must encounter on a regular, unavoidable basis. Everyone has good qualities, even if you have to dig a bit to find them. Ask the Holy Spirit to help you. Maybe you'll end up admiring Joe's passion or persistence. You might discover that he cares deeply about his mother or a particular cause. If you try hard enough, you will find something. When you do, praise God for Joe's unique gift(s). I know, I know. You don't have to feel it. Just do it! Feelings often follow actions.

- *Joe deserves the benefit of the doubt.* It's easy to automatically consign bad intentions to those we dislike. However, we really have no idea what's going on in Joe's head. Maybe he's having a bad day, or a bad year, or even a bad life. It's possible that he craves attention or has a serious self-esteem problem. Who knows? Give him the benefit of the doubt.

- *Joe may be in your life for a reason.* Are you ready for this? God put Joe Annoying in your life to help you get to heaven. Crazy, right? Because God wants to purify us and prepare us for heaven, he sends people like Joe into our lives. Sometimes referred to as "saint makers," these individuals give us an opportunity to practice virtue. Joe was placed in your life to teach you to love unconditionally. Thank God for the gift of Joe. He is helping you to heaven!

- *You are somebody's Joe Annoying.* As hard as it may be to accept, it is very possible that you are as annoying to someone in your life as Joe is annoying to you. Remembering this will help you to look at Joe differently. It might also inspire you to examine your other relationships, to see if there is something *you* need to change!

- *You don't have to like Joe.* Just because the Lord commands us to love one another doesn't mean that we have to become buddies with everyone. Sometimes the best way to love Joe Annoying is to pray for him from a distance. There are some people for whom we have a natural aversion. No matter how much I try, I will probably never become best friends with Joe. That's okay. In no way does it stop me from loving him with an agape love. I may end up really liking Joe at some point, but I shouldn't force it. The Holy Spirit generally softens our hearts gradually.

With the help of the Holy Spirit and the desire to cooperate with his grace, it is possible for us to love everyone with a selfless and unconditional love. We will fail at times but we should keep trying. The Lord doesn't expect us to be perfect, but he does expect us to try.

REMEMBER

1. Love is not a feeling. It is a conscious decision.
2. According to St. Thomas Aquinas, "To love is to will the good of another."

3. Jesus commands us to love with an agape (self-sacrificial) love.

4. If we ask, the Holy Spirit will help us to love as Jesus loves.

5. Sometimes God brings people into our lives who rub us the wrong way . . . to help polish us and equip us for heaven. Thank God for your "Joe Annoying"!

REFLECT

1. Do you struggle to love your enemies (or those who annoy you)?

2. Who is the Joe Annoying in your life? Try to identify two of his good qualities. (Ask the Holy Spirit to help.)

3. Do you pray for the annoying people in your life? Has it changed your feelings for them?

4. How often do you give others the benefit of the doubt?

5. Think of the most offensive person imaginable. It could be someone you know or someone in the news who has committed a terrible crime. Are you willing to pray for them? If so, do it. If not, why not?

RESPOND

Think of someone who drives you crazy or has hurt you, and ask God to bless them today.

LET'S PRAY

Lord Jesus, you and I both know that I don't have what it takes to love my enemies. I am much too self-centered and weak. Through the power of your Holy Spirit, however, I know it is possible. Please activate this power in me and enable me to love as you love. I ask this through the intercession of your Blessed Mother, Mary. Amen.

5

Joy

**I have told you this so that my joy may be in you
and your joy may be complete.
—John 15:11**

Joy is a response to the Lord's presence within us. It is not
dependent on external circumstances. This is a hard concept
to grasp, but one that is life changing. Can you imagine being
filled with joy even in the midst of suffering and chaos? It is
completely possible! Even when your world is crumbling, the
joy of the Holy Spirit lives inside of you. Think about that,
especially if you're suffering right now. You might not feel
it, but the Holy Spirit in you is joyful. Once you tap into that
joy, you can experience it too. No matter how bad things get,
you can choose joy.

When Paul writes about the fruit of joy, he uses the Greek
word *chara*. The same word is used to describe the reaction
of the wise men who saw the star announcing the birth of the
Messiah (Mt 2:10), the feeling experienced by the women who
had just discovered that Jesus rose from the dead (Mt 28:8),
and the apostles' response when Jesus ascended into heaven

(Lk 24:52). The joy given to us as a fruit of the Holy Spirit is more than just run-of-the-mill happiness. It is a powerful gift!

Sometimes we confuse joy and pleasure, which are two different concepts. Pleasure is an involuntary response to favorable external circumstances. It requires no effort on my part. As an example, I enjoy sunny days when the temperature is in the 80s. I don't have to work at it or convince myself to feel happy. It just happens. When the circumstances change (the weather, in this case), the pleasure goes away.

Joy, on the other hand, can be experienced at any time and is not dependent on what is going on around us. Because it is a response to the presence of the Holy Spirit living in us, joy doesn't come and go (unless we let it). The Bible contains several examples of people who were joyful while undergoing serious challenges. Let's look at a few of them so that we can better understand the power of this great fruit of the Holy Spirit.

THE MACEDONIAN CHRISTIANS

Poverty is easily one of the biggest pleasure killers imaginable. I have never experienced extreme poverty, but I do know the pain of looking at a nearly empty bank account and wondering how I will pay my monthly bills. It's hard to imagine being poor and joyful at the same time, but that's exactly how St. Paul describes those in the churches of Macedonia during the first century. Hoping to inspire the church in Corinth (whose members were relatively wealthy) to become more generous, St. Paul praised the impoverished Macedonians, who selflessly contributed to a collection for other needy Christians: "For in a severe test of affliction, the abundance of their joy and their profound poverty overflowed in a wealth of generosity on their part" (2 Cor 8:2).

Amazingly, these individuals had an *abundance of joy* while living in *profound poverty*. Instead of focusing on the unpleasant circumstances in their lives, they chose joy. Think of how our lives would look if we did the same. It would certainly make it easier to deal with bad weather, wouldn't it?

ST. PAUL

St. Paul didn't have it easy either. Let him tell you about his life:

> Five times at the hands of the Jews I received forty lashes minus one. Three times I was beaten with rods, once I was stoned, three times I was shipwrecked, I passed a night and a day on the deep; on frequent journeys, in dangers from rivers, dangers from robbers, dangers from my own race, dangers from Gentiles, dangers in the city, dangers in the wilderness, dangers at sea, dangers among false brothers; in toil and hardship, through many sleepless nights, through hunger and thirst, through frequent fastings, through cold and exposure. (2 Cor 11:24–27)

Wow! I've gone through some bumpy times in my life, but I can't even begin to imagine what Paul endured. He certainly had a right to be miserable, or at least complain a bit, but he didn't. Not only did he refuse to complain, but he also rejoiced in hope: "We even boast of our afflictions, knowing that affliction produces endurance, and endurance, proven character, and proven character, hope, and hope does not disappoint" (Rom 5:3–5).

This was hardly the only time Paul wrote about joy. His letter to the Philippians, which he wrote while under house arrest, is sometimes referred to as the Epistle of Joy. Try to imagine yourself, under arrest and chained to a Roman guard 24/7, saying these words: "Rejoice in the Lord always. I shall say it again: rejoice! Your kindness should be known to all. The Lord is near" (Phil 4:4–5).

When we consider the circumstances under which Paul wrote these words, it's difficult to understand how he could be so positive. For many of us, it's a struggle to find joy when our favorite team loses or it's cold outside. How would we respond if we were imprisoned and awaiting trial in a Roman court? The rest of this Bible passage reveals Paul's secret. He can experience joy in the midst of adversity because "the Lord is at hand." The internal presence of the Holy Spirit makes it possible to rejoice always.

FINDING JOY

So what does this mean for us? Calling on the Holy Spirit is essential, but we have to do some work too. The following recommendations will help you to experience the joy that already exists inside of you. Every one of these suggestions is totally within your power and will cost you nothing, except time. I guarantee that they will be worth the investment.

- *Stop complaining.* It may surprise you, but the most effective way to experience joy is to stop complaining. Not only is this totally under your control, but it also works amazingly well. Griping serves no purpose and is offensive to God. If you can avoid complaining today, you will feel more joy. It's that simple.

- *Count your blessings.* Joy and ingratitude cannot coexist. Unless you find a way to cultivate gratitude, you will not experience the joy of the Holy Spirit. I'll be honest with you. Gratitude does not come naturally for me. I have a tendency to complain, especially about the little annoyances of life. As a result, I have learned to force myself (and that is no exaggeration) to thank God for my blessings when I wake up in the morning. Every day, I thank him for letting me wake up and get out of bed, for having a roof over my head, for my family, for hot water, for food to eat, for my eyesight and hearing, for my relationship with him, and for anything else that may come to mind. Getting into this habit has increased my awareness of the ways God blesses me every day. It works. Try it and see for yourself.

- *Read scripture.* Every time you read the Bible, you have an encounter with the Lord. As a result of that encounter, your joy will increase. According to the prophet Jeremiah, "When I found your words, I devoured them; your words were my joy, the happiness of my heart" (15:16).

    If you're not sure where to start, try the daily Mass readings. They are available online (USCCB.org) or in magazines such as *Magnificat* or *The Word Among Us*. You can also try reading the gospels. I recommend that you start with Mark, which is the shortest gospel. The Acts of the Apostles is also good because it describes how the Holy Spirit worked in the early Church. How much time should you spend? Start with five to ten minutes a day. You can increase that amount over time, but not at the expense of your daily responsibilities. Your disposition can change dramatically by letting the Lord speak to you through the Bible for just a few minutes each day.

- *Live in the moment.* One of the biggest lies we tell ourselves (or Satan tells us) is that we can't experience joy if we are in the midst of an ongoing problem. That is simply not true. I have been faced with some painful long-term problems, such as my daughter's autism, financial issues, and chronic anxiety, and I've still managed to carve out little blocks of happiness. You may not be here tomorrow. The present moment is all you have. Don't waste it by worrying about a future that is not guaranteed. Take a break and enjoy the sunrise, relax with a cup of coffee, take a walk with someone you love, or spend some quiet time with Jesus. By finding joy in the present moment, you are not being irresponsible or burying your head in the sand. Rather, you are obeying Jesus when he commands you, "Do not worry about tomorrow; tomorrow will take care of itself" (Mt 6:34).

- *Stay close to Jesus.* If you make it a point to continually seek Jesus through prayer and the sacraments, you will experience an increase in joy. Going to daily Mass has become a source of great joy for me. It is my refuge in the storm. Being near the Lord has a transformative effect.

The following verse sums up how I feel about this great privilege: "As for me, to be near God is my good; to make the Lord GOD my refuge" (Ps 73:28).

Not everyone can make it to daily Mass, but even attending one or two days during the week will make a difference. Frequent Confession (at least once a month) provides another opportunity to encounter Jesus and can also be a life-changing experience. Time spent with Jesus is never wasted. As the prophet Isaiah reminds us, spending time in the presence of Jesus is a source of joy: "Shout with exultation, City of Zion, for great in your midst is the Holy One of Israel!" (12:6).

- *Recognize the value of trials.* It seems counterintuitive, but learning to appreciate trials can bring you joy. Instead of letting your struggles pull you down, recognize that they can help your faith to grow. According to St. James, "Consider it all joy, my brothers, when you encounter various trials, for you know that the testing of your faith produces perseverance" (1:2–3).

Just before writing this reflection, I discovered that we have a leak in our newly installed roof. This situation definitely has the potential to suck the happiness out of me (it's not the first issue we've encountered with the new roof), but I am choosing to remain joyful. I'm not thrilled about the leak, but I know that this trial can help me to grow in faith. The Holy Spirit knows that this isn't a big deal, and I'm going to ask him to help me handle the situation. I'm not totally on board yet, but I'm starting to feel a little better. Finally, I know I can unite my suffering with the suffering of Jesus. Offering this situation up gives me an opportunity to share in his mission of salvation. Recognizing that truth typically increases our joy.

The joy you seek is inside of you, and nothing that happens in your life can take it away. Looking for joy externally only causes frustration. By consistently following the above suggestions, you will allow the Holy Spirit to work in you and produce lasting joy. It's a process, but it gets easier. Don't give up. The reward is definitely worth it.

REMEMBER

1. Joy is a response to the presence of the Holy Spirit living in us. It is not dependent on external circumstances, but comes from within.

2. Pleasure is a temporary, involuntary response to favorable circumstances.

3. It is possible to experience joy even in the midst of suffering.

4. It is up to us to choose joy over irritation or discouragement.

5. If we stop complaining, count our blessings, read the Bible, live in the moment, stay close to Jesus (through prayer and the sacraments), and recognize the value of trials, we will be on the way to living joyfully.

REFLECT

1. Do you experience joy regularly?

2. What situations typically rob you of joy? Name two or three.

3. When you lose your joy, what steps do you normally take to regain it?

4. Are you able to enjoy moments of joy even though you may have unresolved problems in your life?

5. How often does worrying about the future rob you of today's happiness? Do you feel that such worrying is a productive use of your time?

RESPOND

Make the decision that you will not complain about anything today. Ask the Holy Spirit to help you remember your promise.

LET'S PRAY

Dear Holy Spirit, thank you for walking through life with me. I know that you are always joyful, even when I am not. Grant me the grace to choose joy, even when facing trials and suffering. Amen.

6

Peace

Peace I leave with you; my peace I give to you.
—John 14:27

If you had to choose only one fruit of the Holy Spirit, which
one would it be? My guess is that most of us would choose
peace. It's something we all crave. I travel from coast to coast,
helping people to achieve this sought-after prize, which is
often perceived as an unreachable goal. But here's the good
news for those who continue to seek an oasis of peace in their
chaotic lives: We don't have to run around looking for peace.
That is a discouraging (and totally false) belief.

The truth revealed in scripture (Jn 14:27) is that Jesus
left us the peace we seek. Through the Holy Spirit, the peace
we are trying to find is already ours. We just have to realize
it and claim it.

SO . . . WHAT IS PEACE?

Sometimes we equate peace with the absence of conflict;
however, the peace that flows from the Holy Spirit does not
depend on the elimination of external difficulties. In discussing the fruit of peace, St. Paul uses the Greek word *eirene*,

which implies a sense of serenity or tranquility. Peace "keeps the mind untroubled in the face of spiritual or temporal trials."[5] No matter what is taking place around you, it is possible to experience peace.

I can personally vouch for the fact that it is possible to be at peace even when your world seems to be falling apart. After struggling with infertility for the first few years of our marriage, Eileen and I learned in 1997 that she was pregnant. We were ecstatic. A few months later, an ultrasound revealed that we were having twin girls. I didn't think it was possible for us to be even happier, but we were. That happiness didn't last long. A few hours after returning home from the ultrasound, Eileen got a call from her doctor. He had detected a serious problem with the girls and wanted to see us the next day. We didn't know much more than that. We speculated on what the problem could be and tried not to think about it. That didn't work. We spent the remainder of the night worrying about the situation and praying for a positive outcome.

The following day we received some devastating news. Our twins were suffering from a life-threatening condition known as twin-to-twin transfusion syndrome. The doctor told us bluntly that without treatment they had only a 10 percent chance of being born alive. To make matters even worse, treatment options were practically nonexistent at this point in the pregnancy.

I can still remember sitting there, holding Eileen's hand, trying to compose myself and think of a question to ask. My mind was blank. I never expected to be in this situation. Once Eileen became pregnant, I was so happy to be free from infertility issues that I never even considered something like this.

We were told to come back on Monday (it was Friday) for further evaluation. As we prepared to leave, the doctor said, "If something happens over the weekend, it's not your fault. You're doing all you can." At that point, any illusion of this not being an emergency situation instantly vanished.

Eileen and I didn't say much on the drive home. We were both stunned. As much as I wanted to comfort her, I didn't know what to say. It was a beautiful day, but that didn't matter to me. All I could feel was an empty, gnawing ache in my stomach. That evening we informed our family of the prognosis, and many of them promised to pray. I knew in my head that God can do all things, but I didn't feel it in my heart. Nonetheless, Eileen and I made the decision that we would pray and try not to lose hope.

We went to daily Mass on Saturday morning and something special happened. My mother-in-law was there (Betty was a great person with a very strong faith), and she approached us after Mass with her friend Rosemary. The two of them spent much of their time in church and believed strongly in the healing power of God. Rosemary presented us with a card indicating that she had spent an hour praying for us before the Blessed Sacrament. As we thanked her, she assured us that this was the first of many hours she would spend in prayer for us. Suddenly, for the first time since getting the bad news, I felt a slight hint of peace.

As the weeks passed, Eileen and I continued to hope and pray. Fully aware that the girls could die at any moment, we forced ourselves to live one day at a time. We did what we could to let the need be known, so people could be praying for us; yet we also understood that the matter was ultimately in

God's hands. We were not "super-saints" with an unshakable faith, however; we trusted because we had no choice. The situation was so dire that God was our only hope. Fighting through the desire to take charge and fix everything, we surrendered control of the situation to the Lord. As a result, we experienced his peace. I am happy to report that Mary and Elizabeth did survive and are now healthy young adults. God is so good!

ST. PAUL'S SIX-STEP PLAN FOR PEACE

That it is possible to experience peace even in the midst of difficult circumstances is apparent in St. Paul's letter to the Philippians. Even though he was a prisoner when he wrote this letter, Paul chose to rejoice. We discussed the first part of the following passage in the last chapter, but I'm including it again here because it fits so well:

> Rejoice in the Lord always. I shall say it again: rejoice! Your kindness should be known to all. The Lord is near. Have no anxiety at all, but in everything, by prayer and petition, with thanksgiving, make your requests known to God. Then the peace of God that surpasses all understanding will guard your hearts and minds in Christ Jesus. (Phil 4:4–7)

Since the main focus of my ministry is overcoming anxiety, I can't remember a time when I didn't use this Bible passage in one of my parish missions, talks, or retreats. It contains the secret of finding peace in the midst of the storm.

In this passage, Paul lists six steps that can deliver us from stress and fill us with the Lord's peace:

1. *Rejoice.* As we discussed in the last chapter, joy is a choice. You can choose to rejoice, even when faced with external struggles. Joy is a response to the Lord's presence within us. If you are looking for peace, get into the habit of rejoicing. If you don't feel like it, do it anyway. Why should you rejoice when things are going wrong in your life? Let's look at step 2.

2. *Recognize God's presence.* No matter where you are or what is happening in your life, the Lord is with you. You received the Holy Spirit at Baptism, and if you are not in a state of serious sin, he lives inside of you. And, since the Trinity can't be divided, the Father and the Son are right there too. Because of the Lord's presence, St. Paul can rejoice while imprisoned and you can rejoice as you deal with your own personal struggles.

3. *Don't worry.* I've written and spoken about this, but more importantly, I continue to practice it every day. I can assure you that it is possible to avoid worry. Unlike fear, which is an uncontrollable emotion, worry is a conscious decision. You can't stop yourself from being afraid, but you can stop yourself from worrying. The easiest and most effective way is to do something else instead. What can you do? The next step contains a great suggestion . . .

4. *Pray.* Here's something to remember: You can't worry and pray at the same time. You can be afraid while you pray, but it's not possible to worry and pray simultaneously.

The moment you begin to present your requests to God (as recommended by St. Paul), you have ceased worrying and commenced praying. Pretty cool, isn't it? Prayer is a productive use of your time. Worry is not.

5. *Be thankful.* Note that Paul doesn't recommend thanking God after our prayers are answered. He instructs us to pray "with thanksgiving," which is something totally different. Thanking God in advance implies total confidence that he hears us and will answer in the best way possible. Jesus told us to "ask and it will be given to you" (Mt 7:7), and that's why we can pray in this way. You don't have to feel it. Just follow the advice of Jesus and St. Paul and say thank you.

6. *Receive God's peace.* If we take Paul's advice and present our needs to the Lord, we can expect to receive the supernatural peace that sustains us. It sounds simple, but I guarantee that it works. This is how Eileen and I managed to be at peace while she was pregnant with our twins. We surrendered everything to the Lord, and he gave us the gift of peace. We left the details up to him. Even though we didn't know how the situation would turn out, we believed that the Lord would do what's best. We didn't always feel it, but we did believe it. We made the decision to trust, but the peace that resulted came entirely from him.

PEACE BLOCKERS

At this point, I have to tell you something that you might not want to hear. It is entirely possible to follow St. Paul's instructions and not experience peace. It has happened to me many times, so don't be alarmed if it happens to you too. In no way does it mean that prayer is ineffective or that God isn't listening. Typically, it indicates one of two things. The good news is that both of these situations can be corrected.

First, we must consider if there is any serious, unconfessed sin in our life. If this is the case, all the prayer in the world will not bring about peace. Through the sacrament of Reconciliation, however, we can receive forgiveness for our sins and remove any obstacles that block us from being filled with God's peace. There is no sin too great to be forgiven, but we must take action. To get results, we must confess our sins to a priest and express a firm desire to avoid committing them again in the future. I know from personal experience that carrying around serious sin causes misery. Do yourself a favor and take advantage of God's abundant outpouring of mercy in Confession.

If serious sin is not the issue, it could be that there is a problem with the way that you're praying. Let's begin with the age-old question—is there a wrong way to pray? Strictly speaking, the answer is no. Any communication between you and God is a good thing. Sometimes people get so hung up on saying the "right words" that they stop praying entirely. Don't let that happen. Even if you don't know what to say, make it a point to speak to the Lord every day. "I don't know what to say to you" is actually the beginning of a prayer! But if there is a problem with the way you are praying, you may not experience the peace promised by St. Paul.

Here's an example. After my conversion experience, I became convinced that the Lord was calling me to become a permanent deacon. Doing so, I believed, would allow me to effectively lead others to him and also advance my own holiness. That was my plan, and it made perfect sense. However, I never bothered to ask the Lord if it's what *he* wanted. After all, with so many people rejecting him, why would he say no if I wanted to serve him as an ordained minister? So, I decided to call my pastor and let him know the good news. He knew that I attended daily Mass and participated in church activities, and I was convinced that he'd be thrilled when I told him. In no way did I anticipate his reaction.

To say that he was not enthusiastic about my decision was an understatement. He expressed concern that the diaconate formation would take me away from my family responsibilities. Even though he had a point (my girls were young, and my wife did need my help around the house), I was devastated. Believing that my pastor was wrong, I asked the Lord to validate my decision in another way. We had three permanent deacons in our parish, and I was friends with each of them. I prayed that one or more of them would recommend that I pursue the diaconate. This would give me the confirmation I needed and would help to change our pastor's mind.

Nothing happened.

Days turned into weeks, but I refused to let go of my dream. I prayed every day that "something" would happen and the door would open for me. Needless to say, I was miserable. I looked forward to the day when my daughters would be older and I could pursue "my calling." It's embarrassing to admit, but I even started looking at some of the other men in my parish and prayed that none of them got "my" deacon slot before I was ready. I was definitely praying (as St. Paul recommended), but I felt no peace.

Here's the problem. My prayer was all about me and not about God. I was praying that my will, not his, be done. My selfishness didn't give the Lord room to work. I knew what I wanted and wouldn't be happy until I received it. Praying like that will never bring us peace.

It took a while, but I eventually realized my problem and accepted the Lord's decision. And I'm glad I did because his plan was much better than mine. Although I have not been ordained a deacon, I have shared the Gospel with thousands of souls through my parish missions, talks, books, and radio shows. Once I stopped fighting him, God was able to work in my life and grant me the peace I sought.

FOCUS ON JESUS

If I could give you only one suggestion for experiencing greater peace, it would be this—stay focused on Jesus. More than anything else, that will give you the peace you seek. Concentrating on your problems will lead to increased worry and decreased peace. Focusing on Jesus, however, will fill you with hope. No matter what problem I'm faced with, spending some time reading the gospels always makes me feel better. It may take some time, but I always end up being at peace. The prophet Isaiah summarized this concept nicely: "With firm purpose you maintain peace; in peace, because of our trust in you" (26:3).

As you get to know Jesus better, you will see that he was all about doing the will of his Father (Jn 6:38). Learning to imitate him will put you on the road to peace. Never hesitate to ask God for what you need, but be sure to pray like Jesus prayed. On the night before he died, Jesus prayed that the cup of suffering would pass him by. But with the words "Thy will be done," he surrendered to the Father's will. If you can learn to pray that way, you too will find yourself at peace no matter what is going on around you.

REMEMBER

1. Peace is a sense of tranquility that keeps the mind untroubled in the face of spiritual or temporal trials.

2. The peace given by the Holy Spirit does not depend on the absence of conflict in our life.

3. To experience the Lord's peace, we must surrender to his will.

4. It is impossible to worry and pray simultaneously.

5. When we pray and still don't experience peace, it typically means that we either have serious, unconfessed sin in our life or are not open to God's will.

REFLECT

1. Did you ever experience peace during a time of crisis? Explain.

2. When things go wrong, what is your first reaction—to worry or to turn to God? Which brings more peace?

3. Recall a time that your prayer wasn't answered. Think of one or two reasons why it may have been a blessing.

4. Are you willing to surrender your current intentions to God's will? If not, why not?

5. Why is it important for us to be at peace? How can it help others?

RESPOND

What is robbing you of peace today? Ask the Lord to resolve the situation in the best way possible, and ask him to fill you with his peace.

LET'S PRAY

Dear Father, you are the giver of all good things. I ask you to hear and grant my intentions today, but only if they align with your will. Please fill me with the peace that flows from your Holy Spirit. In Jesus' name. Amen.

7

Patience

> But do not ignore this one fact, beloved, that with
> the Lord one day is like a thousand years and a
> thousand years like one day.
> **—2 Peter 3:8**

"God, grant me patience . . . and I want it *now*!" Sound familiar?

Blame it on growing up in a fast-food culture, or simply the fact that I am a bit of a control freak: When I want something, I don't like to wait. That tendency has created much frustration for me over the years, as God has—slowly—taught me to be patient.

Like it or not, waiting is a part of life. We can either find a way to deal with it or live in a constant state of irritation. A naturally impatient person like me needs a lot of assistance. Fortunately, I discovered someone who could help me—the Holy Spirit.

To bear the fruit of patience requires some effort. Sure, the Holy Spirit is willing to do the bulk of the work, but we still have to yield control. Let's look at four practical applications—patience with God, patience with circumstances, patience with others, and patience with ourselves. If we can learn to be patient in each of these areas, our lives will be transformed.

PATIENCE WITH GOD

> Be still before the LORD; wait for him.
>
> —**Psalm 37:7**

Being patient with God is something I struggle with every day. Because I tend to be controlling, it drives me crazy to remain still and wait. When I have a need, my natural tendency is to do whatever I can to fix it. Even if what I'm doing is not productive, it helps me to feel like I'm in control. But, as much as I may be comforted by acting in this way, it will get me nowhere. I cannot grow close to God without surrendering control of my life to him. This means that I must make a conscious decision to trust him. Sooner or later, I'll have to stop running around and wait for him to act. That requires patience.

Someone once told me that it's a good thing God isn't in charge of a fire department. He definitely operates according to his own schedule, doesn't he? I'm sure you've seen this in your life, but we can also find examples in the Bible. When Adam and Eve disobeyed God, he promised to send a Messiah (Gn 3:15) to repair the damage. Wouldn't you think that he would act on such an urgent need ASAP? Yet it took thousands of years for Jesus to arrive on the scene. Then he came into the world as an infant, and another thirty years passed before he began his ministry. The culmination of God's plan—the Passion, Death, and Resurrection of his beloved Son—occurred only after thousands of years of waiting, thirty years of preparation, and three years of public ministry.

If God had asked me for advice, I might have suggested that this was an urgent situation, that we needed to get it done faster. (Oddly enough, he never asked for my advice.) Instead, the Incarnation, God's most powerful self-revelation to the world, was accomplished in "the fullness of time," as we read in Paul's letter to the Galatians: "But when the fullness of time had come, God sent his Son, born of a woman, born under the law, to ransom those under the law, so that we might receive adoption" (4:4–5).

Of course, when I urge you to have patience with God, that doesn't mean to sit back and wait passively for God to fix your problems without any effort on your part. God expects us to do what we can. Praying for the ability to pay our monthly bills without looking for a job is not good. The Lord gives us common sense and skills for a reason.

However, if we've said our prayers and done everything in our power and the problem remains, he is asking us to be patient and trust him. It might not be easy, but it will help us grow closer to him. We should keep praying and doing what we can, but also give him some time to work. He will come through when the time is right.

PATIENCE WITH CIRCUMSTANCES

Rejoice in hope, endure in affliction, persevere in prayer.

—**Romans 12:12**

If it was up to me, every day would be sunny and warm. I would never get sick or feel tired. My car would not break down, and home repairs would be unnecessary. There would be no danger of running out of money. I would eliminate all suffering from my life. After all, who likes to suffer?

Here's the thing: As much as I dislike suffering, some of my greatest spiritual growth has occurred during trials and difficulties. Let me give you an example. After encountering Jesus in the storm and surrendering my life to him, I wanted to share the Good News on a full-time basis. I was never that excited about my job as a software developer, but after getting involved with blogging and Catholic radio, I just knew that I had found my calling. *No more of this software stuff for me.*

My prayers sounded something like this: "It's obvious that I'm supposed to be working full time for you, Lord. Let's make it happen." Nothing happened. The Lord provided more opportunities to speak about him on Catholic radio, but nothing that generated income. I was stuck at my day job and absolutely hated it!

For close to three years, I complained to the Lord every day about how much I disliked my job. It made no sense that he wasn't responding to my prayers. "I don't want this for me, Lord. I want to do this for you!" Still no response. In fact, things got worse for me. Now, instead of developing software, I was balancing budgets and managing employees. In my mind, there was no way I could ever be happy unless I got out of this job and into full-time ministry. I was willing to try anything.

Taking the advice of a friend, I made the decision to consecrate myself entirely to Jesus through Mary, using the method popularized by St. Louis de Montfort. On September 4, 2011, I began the thirty-three days of preparation and hoped for the best.

Shortly after formally consecrating my life on October 7 (the Feast of Our Lady of the Rosary), my prayers were answered in an unexpected way. No, I didn't get my long-anticipated full-time job working for the Lord; it was something much more subtle. While taking my dog for a walk, I got a strong feeling of peace about my current situation. This unexpected contentment prompted me to say (and truly mean), "Lord, if you want me to stay at my current job, it's fine with me."

I couldn't believe the words that came out of my mouth. What was more impressive, I actually meant it! Finally, through the intercession of the Blessed Mother, I was able to surrender my desires to the Lord.

In a matter of weeks, I was suddenly laid off and got my start in full-time ministry. I didn't realize it then, but my time in the desert helped me to get to know the Lord better. Looking back now, I understand that the desire to work in full-time ministry was coming from him, after all. He was just waiting for me to fully surrender my will before he allowed it to happen. This frustrating set of circumstances enabled me to get to know Jesus (and Mary) better and gave me the opportunity to put into practice the words "Thy will be done."

Instead of growing impatient about the circumstances in your life, ask the Lord what he's trying to teach you. He knows what he's doing.

PATIENCE WITH OTHERS

> The ill-tempered stir up strife, but the patient settle disputes.
>
> —**Proverbs 15:18**

It's not about you. Pastor Rick Warren used these four words to open his best-selling book—*The Purpose-Driven Life.*[6] It's a message that we as Christians should never forget, though we do just that every time we lose our patience with another person.

Impatience is a clear sign of self-centeredness. Whenever I grow impatient with someone, it is absolutely about me. When someone moves too slowly, disregards my opinion, chews their gum too loudly, or takes too long to tell a story, I often grow impatient. Why? Mainly because I have determined that they are violating my self-declared right to an annoyance-free life.

One of the best ways to become more patient with others is to reflect on how patient God is with us. Heck, I lose my patience at the cashier who takes too long to ring up the customer in front of me, but Jesus remains patient with me even though my sins put him on the Cross! I can argue all I want that "these people" are the reason that I lose my patience, but I don't have a leg to stand on. If Jesus is patient with me, I better find a way to be patient with others.

As you begin to exercise patience with others, however, you may fall into a common trap: losing patience with *impatient people.* Just like the ex-smoker who never passes up an opportunity to preach about the evils of tobacco, or the reformed sugarholic who can't resist criticizing your chocolate cake photo on Facebook, those who have learned to cultivate patience are often quick to denounce that particular weakness in others. I should know. This is something I struggle with constantly. It sounds silly, but I often lose my patience with those who are impatient.

In striving to remain patient we are imitating Jesus, who always managed to exhibit patience and restraint. When a Samaritan village refused to receive him (Lk 9:52–56), James and John asked, "Lord, do you want us to call down fire from heaven to consume them?" The Lord rebuked them, and they moved on to another village. Instead of being confrontational with someone trying our patience, sometimes it's best to just walk away and pray for the person from a distance.

PATIENCE WITH OURSELVES

> That I might not become too elated, a thorn in the flesh was given to me, an angel of Satan, to beat me, to keep me from being too elated. Three times I begged the Lord about this, that it might leave me, but he said to me, "My grace is sufficient for you, for power is made perfect in weakness."
>
> —2 Corinthians 12:7–9

Even St. Paul had to be patient in overcoming his own areas of weakness. Can you relate to this? Do you find it difficult to be patient with your own flaws and quirks? I do. Once I recognize a bad habit in my life (I have many to choose from) and I ask the Lord to help me overcome it, I expect it to be gone yesterday! That is an unrealistic mindset and will only cause frustration.

So, what can we do as we await our personal transformation? Here are a few things I've found helpful.

- *Remember that sanctification takes time.* Just as you're called to be patient with those around you, you must learn to be patient with yourself. God is in charge of the sanctification process, and he typically changes us gradually. By trying to speed things up, we attempt to take control of the situation. Let God be God. He knows what he's doing!

- *Don't give in to discouragement.* Over the years, my mouth has caused a great deal of pain for those around me. I have a tendency to be sarcastic and to attack others with my words. Even though I know this is a problem and I have prayed about it, I still mess up. In the past, I would get very upset and feel defeated when I acted this way despite my good intentions. Believing that I would never conquer this bad habit, I wondered why I should even try to improve. Without realizing it, I was playing into Satan's hands. He loves it when we stop trying to conquer our sinful habits. Don't make the mistake of falling for his lies.

- *Stay close to the sacraments.* The Lord sometimes allows us to fall because he wants us to recognize that we need his help. The next time you fall into sin, apologize to God (and the person you offended), ask for the grace to do better next time, and go to Confession. Receive the Eucharist as often as possible. Doing so will be infinitely more effective than wallowing in self-pity and hopelessness.

- *Be ready for God's "pop quiz."* If you are striving to become more patient, you can expect the Lord to send along people who will try your patience. You will also find your-self in situations that frustrate you and force you to wait. Keep praying for the assistance of the Holy Spirit and do your best to cooperate with the grace that he gives you. Above all, be patient, especially with yourself. It takes time *and patience* to become patient!

REMEMBER

1. To bear the fruit of patience requires some effort on our part. The Holy Spirit is willing to do the bulk of the work, but we have to yield control.

2. We must learn to be patient with God, circumstances, others, and ourselves.

3. Being patient with God means we must trust in his timing.

4. The Lord often uses unpleasant circumstances to draw us closer to him.

5. When we are trying to become more patient, God will sometimes allow us to fall. He wants us to recognize that we need his help.

REFLECT

1. Is it most difficult for you to be patient with God, with circumstances, with others, or with yourself? Why?

2. Besides asking for the help of the Holy Spirit (which is a given), how can you work on becoming more patient with what you identified in question 1?

3. Who is the most patient person you know? How do you feel when you are around that person?

4. How do you typically react when you lose your patience? What can you do to improve your chances of remaining patient next time?

5. Who is more affected when you are patient, you or those around you? Why?

RESPOND

Look for at least one concrete opportunity to be patient today and act on it. It may involve offering up time sitting in traffic, listening attentively to a story from a long-winded friend, affirming your trust in God's timing, or refusing to get discouraged in your spiritual progress. If you can't decide, ask God to place you in a situation that allows you to practice patience.

LET'S PRAY

Dear Jesus, grant me the grace to be patient with you, with circumstances, with others, and with myself. When I fail, please forgive me and grant me the grace to get up and try again. I ask this in your mighty name. Amen.

8

Kindness

Love is patient, love is kind.
—1 Corinthians 13:4

Sometimes we think that kindness is all about being "nice" or having good feelings toward others. It's actually about being merciful. In fact, kindness is mercy in action. Although we sin repeatedly, God is always willing to give us another chance. That is kindness. It is characterized by patience and mercy, and it flows from his unconditional love.

KINDNESS ACCORDING TO ST. PAUL

In his list of the Spirit's fruits, St. Paul uses the Greek word *chrestotes* to denote kindness. It's a word that he uses several other places in his writings. Taking a look at some of those other instances will give us insight into what he means by kindness. In the second chapter of Romans, we read: "Do you suppose, then, you who judge those who engage in such things and yet do them yourself, that you will escape the judgment of God? Or do you hold his priceless kindness, forbearance, and patience in low esteem, unaware that the kindness of God would lead you to repentance?" (Rom 2:3–4).

In this passage, Paul reminds the Romans of God's extreme patience and mercy toward them. Even though they were acting in a way that displeased the Lord, he was giving them time to repent. Instead of being thankful, however, they were passing judgment on others. Paul wanted the Romans to understand that the Lord wasn't letting them off the hook because they were special. He was doing it out of mercy. They would still be judged for their actions one day, but they were being granted a temporary reprieve. In his kindness, the Lord was giving them a chance to get their act together and repent.

Later in the same book, Paul uses the same word three more times in one verse: "See, then, the kindness and severity of God: severity toward those who fell, but God's kindness to you, provided you remain in his kindness; otherwise you too will be cut off" (Rom 11:22). Once again, Paul is urging the Gentile Christians to be grateful for the opportunity to make things right with God, and to remember that the Lord's kindness and forbearance won't last forever. They (and we) should be careful not to take the Lord's kindness for granted.

The kindness shown by the Lord is a total gift. In no way have we earned it or deserve it. His mercy and kindness flow from the unconditional love that he has for each of us, as we read in this passage from Titus:

> For we ourselves were once foolish, disobedient, deluded, slaves to various desires and pleasures, living in malice and envy, hateful ourselves and hating one another. But when the kindness and

generous love of God our savior appeared, not because of any righteous deeds we had done but because of his mercy, he saved us through the bath of rebirth and renewal by the holy Spirit, whom he richly poured out on us through Jesus Christ our savior, so that we might be justified by his grace and become heirs in hope of eternal life. (Ti 3:3–7)

In his letter to the church at Colossae, Paul challenges us even more. Being grateful for the Lord's kindness is only the beginning. We are also called to show the same kindness to others: "Put on then, as God's chosen ones, holy and beloved, heartfelt compassion, kindness, humility, gentleness, and patience, bearing with one another and forgiving one another, if one has a grievance against another; as the Lord has forgiven you, so must you also do" (Col 3:12–13).

KINDNESS IN THE OLD TESTAMENT

In the book of Genesis, the sons of Jacob were forced to travel to Egypt years after selling their brother Joseph into slavery (Gn 37:28), to obtain food during a famine. They were unaware that Joseph had risen to a position of great power and was in charge of the food supply. Since many years had passed and Joseph spoke to his brothers in Egyptian (using an interpreter), they failed to recognize him.

When Joseph eventually revealed his identity, the men flung themselves at his feet. They fully expected revenge. Instead, Joseph chose to respond with kindness: "'Do not fear. Can I take the place of God? Even though you meant harm to me, God meant it for good, to achieve this present end, the survival of many people. So now, do not fear. I will provide for you and for your children.' By thus speaking kindly to them, he reassured them" (Gn 50:19–21). Joseph had the power to make his brothers suffer for what they did to him, but he chose to treat them mercifully. He could have gotten revenge by sending them away empty-handed or throwing them in prison. Instead he honored his God and chose the way of peace for himself and his family.

Then and now, the way of kindness is the way of mercy and peace—not just for ourselves, but for everyone it touches.

PAYING IT FORWARD

Shortly after I started driving, I was traveling home from the store one evening and had to merge onto a major highway. Since the traffic was moving at a fast pace, I knew that I couldn't waste time once I made my move. There was a car in front of me trying to merge, and I patiently waited for my turn to go.

The car ahead of me started to move forward, and I looked over my shoulder to survey the oncoming traffic. After a few seconds, I saw a break in the traffic and decided to go for it. Still looking back at the traffic, I stepped on the gas and floored it. CRASH! I turned my head to the front, and saw the last thing I wanted to see. Remember that car ahead of me that had started to move? Apparently, the driver had second thoughts and decided to wait. You guessed it. I plowed right into his car.

Since it was dark and we were in the middle of the on ramp, the other car drove forward and pulled over on the shoulder of the road. I was so terrified that I briefly entertained the thought of speeding away and taking my chances. A few seconds later, my conscience kicked in and I pulled behind the other car and got out. This was my first accident, and I didn't know what to expect.

Fortunately, the other driver was remarkably calm. I apologized profusely, and we exchanged insurance information and phone numbers. While I can't recall the details of our conversation, I vividly remember the fact that he wasn't nasty at all. Both of our cars were drivable, but his trunk was seriously damaged. Very much rattled, I drove home and prepared to face my father. I wasn't sure what he would say, but I knew it wasn't going to be pleasant.

As expected, my father informed me of the negative consequences that could result from the accident. As the days passed, I grew increasingly fearful. I anticipated hearing the worst about increased insurance rates, medical costs, and other horrible possibilities that my father planted in my head. One night, the phone rang and it was the other driver. My heart raced as he began to speak.

The night of the accident, he was on the way home from the supermarket and had groceries in his trunk. Because of the damage, he couldn't open the trunk and most of the food spoiled. When I apologized again, he told me not to worry about it. All he cared about was getting his car repaired. He told me that he felt fine and asked if I was okay.

Then, very casually, he told me something else. Early in his driving career, someone gave him a break when he plowed into them. Now he was paying it forward. I was incredibly grateful. He could have caused a lot of trouble for me, but he chose to practice kindness instead.

As a fruit of the Holy Spirit, kindness is a powerful virtue that can transform lives. When we are kind to those we encounter, it can affect the way they treat others. It's no exaggeration to say that kindness can change the world.

How can I say that? Well, forty years after that first car accident, on April 3, 2019, I was involved in another, far more serious accident. As I traveled on the Pennsylvania Turnpike at 70 mph, I noticed that the drivers in front of me were applying their brakes. I did the same and ended up coming to a complete stop. Instinctively, I glanced in my rearview mirror and saw a car speeding toward me. It did not appear to be slowing down, and I braced for what was about to happen.

My car was hit from behind and slammed into the concrete divider, bouncing a few times before coming to a stop facing the oncoming traffic. Miraculously, I was able to drive the car to the shoulder of the road. My car was totaled, but I survived (with a few aches and pains).

The other driver pulled over behind me, and I could see that he was a young man. Even though I was dazed, I had a flashback to the time another driver was merciful to me because someone was merciful to him. It was now time for me to do the same thing. Shortly thereafter, the state police arrived and handled all the details. I never spoke to the young man who hit me, but I did pray for him. I knew that he was probably sweating it out, wondering what I would do. Even though the accident was totally his fault, I was not angry.

In the days that followed, I received lots of advice about lawyers, inconvenience, and retribution. Several people told me that I shouldn't have to suffer because someone else was careless. But I kept thinking about the driver who showed mercy to me decades ago. My deductible was covered, I received a settlement for my totaled car, and I was alive. Case closed. The Holy Spirit worked through me, and I was able to be merciful.

DIVINE MERCY

When we show kindness to others, we are mirroring God's mercy. Therefore, any look at the fruit of kindness would be incomplete without a brief overview of the Divine Mercy message.

The Catholic devotion to Divine Mercy is most associated with St. Maria Faustina Kowalska (1905–1938), a Polish nun known as the "Secretary of Divine Mercy" for her famous *Diary*, in which she records the words of Jesus, who appeared to her in a series of apparitions beginning in 1931. He reminded Faustina that God loves us and that his mercy is greater than our sins. While this was not a new message, these words brought new life to the Gospel message at a time when people desperately needed to be reminded of the infinite mercy of God. Here, in an excerpt from St. Faustina's *Diary*, Jesus reveals the power of Divine Mercy:

> Let the greatest sinners place their trust in My mercy. They have the right before others to trust in the abyss of My mercy. My daughter, write about my mercy towards tormented souls. Souls

> that make an appeal to My mercy delight Me. To
> such souls I grant even more graces than they
> ask. I cannot punish even the greatest sinner if he
> makes an appeal to My compassion, but on the
> contrary, I justify him in my unfathomable and
> inscrutable mercy. Write: before I come as a just
> Judge, I first open wide the door of My mercy.
> He who refuses to pass through the door of My
> mercy must pass through the door of My justice.[7]

The words of Jesus to St. Faustina echo St. Paul's writings to the Romans. Because he is kind and merciful, the Lord is giving us the chance to escape his justice. To do so, however, we must respond to his kindness and accept the offer. And because the Lord understands that we have a tendency to put things off, he emphasizes the importance of acting now. The offer won't last forever. He wants us to take it seriously. For more information about the message of Divine Mercy, visit the website of the Marian Fathers of the Immaculate Conception of the Most Blessed Virgin Mary (TheDivineMercy.org).

JESUS TEACHES US ABOUT KINDNESS

How can we imitate God and exhibit the fruit of kindness in our daily lives? In the parable of the Good Samaritan, Jesus spells out exactly what we need to do:

> There was a scholar of the law who stood up to
> test him and said, "Teacher, what must I do to
> inherit eternal life?" Jesus said to him, "What
> is written in the law? How do you read it?" He
> said in reply, "You shall love the Lord, your God,

> with all your heart, with all your being, with all your strength, and with all your mind, and your neighbor as yourself." He replied to him, "You have answered correctly; do this and you will live." (Lk 10:25–28)

Most observant Jews understood the law, but Jesus was about to kick it up a notch. When the lawyer asked, "And who is my neighbor?" Jesus responded by telling the parable:

> A man fell victim to robbers as he went down from Jerusalem to Jericho. They stripped and beat him and went off leaving him half-dead. A priest happened to be going down that road, but when he saw him, he passed by on the opposite side. Likewise a Levite came to the place, and when he saw him, he passed by on the opposite side. But a Samaritan traveler who came upon him was moved with compassion at the sight. He approached the victim, poured oil and wine over his wounds and bandaged them. Then he lifted him up on his own animal, took him to an inn and cared for him. The next day he took out two silver coins and gave them to the innkeeper with the instruction, "Take care of him. If you spend more than what I have given you, I shall repay you on my way back." (Lk 10:30–35)

After telling the story, Jesus posed a question to the lawyer. It's obvious from his answer that he got the point of the parable.

> "Which of these three, in your opinion, was
> neighbor to the robbers' victim?" He answered,
> "The one who treated him with mercy." Jesus said
> to him, "Go and do likewise." (Lk 10:36–37)

Always remember that kindness involves doing something. We are challenged not only to feel compassion for our neighbor but also to alleviate his suffering by taking action. We take action by being kind and merciful. If it sounds difficult, that's because it is. Actually, it's just about impossible. Jesus knew this, and that's why he gave us the Holy Spirit. Suddenly, the impossible becomes possible!

REMEMBER

1. Kindness is the quality of conveying sympathy and concern for those in trouble or need. It is shown in generosity of conduct and forgiveness of injuries sustained.

2. Kindness is mercy in action.

3. God loves us, and his mercy is greater than our sins.

4. Because he is kind and merciful, the Lord gives us the chance to escape his justice. To do so, we must accept his mercy.

5. The Lord expects us to imitate him by being kind to those around us. To do this, we must rely on the power of the Holy Spirit.

REFLECT

1. Recall some specific instances where you have experienced God's kindness in your life.

2. Have you ever been treated unkindly by others? How did it feel?

3. Can you remember any occasions where you treated others unkindly? Did you attempt to repair the damage? If not, what can you do to make amends today?

4. Read the parable of the Good Samaritan (Lk 10:25–37), and put yourself in the place of the lawyer. How would you respond to Jesus' instruction to show mercy to your neighbor? Identify someone in your life who is that neighbor in need. How will you help them today?

5. Why do you think that we often fail to show kindness to others? What specific steps can we take to remedy the situation?

RESPOND

Be kind to someone today by giving them the last word in an argument, doing a favor for them (without their knowledge), listening to their problems, or forgiving a past offense.

LET'S PRAY

Merciful and loving Father, thank you for the kindness you show me every day. I want to show the same kindness to others. If I try to do this through my own power, I know I will fail. Please grant me the grace to be kind to those around me. With the help of your Holy Spirit, I know I can succeed. I ask this in Jesus' name. Amen.

9

Goodness

Trust in the LORD and do good.
—Psalm 37:3

As a teenager, I discovered the joy of stamp collecting. After receiving a starter kit and price guide for Christmas, in a relatively short period of time I built a large collection of stamps from around the world. While it was exciting to collect postage stamps from foreign countries, nothing thrilled me as much as acquiring American stamps from the 1920s through the 1940s.

I would purchase a "grab bag" of vintage US postage stamps at local department stores for a very reasonable price. These assortments contained a variety of stamps from the past. Because you couldn't see inside the package, it was always fun to discover which stamps were contained inside. One of my neighborhood friends was also into stamp collecting, and we often traded items from our collections. I would typically look up the value of the stamps in my price guide before we agreed on a trade, to ensure that nobody was getting cheated.

One day, as my buddy was showing me some recent acquisitions, I was blown away by what I saw. He had a 1927 Charles Lindbergh *Spirit of St. Louis* airmail stamp! This stamp was special for two reasons. First, it marked the very first time that a living person was honored on a US postage stamp. Second, it was rectangular and much larger than any other stamp in my collection. I knew that I had to have it, and I proposed a trade.

My friend seemed willing to make the deal. Before he committed, however, he asked me to look up its value in my price guide. As I paged through the guide and located the stamp in question, my heart sank. It was worth over five dollars, which was a big deal to kids like us. I wanted this stamp badly, but I knew that he wouldn't agree to the trade once I told him how much the stamp was worth. So I lied about the value of the stamp, and we made the trade.

I would like to tell you that I didn't realize what I did was wrong, but that's simply not true. I knew exactly what I should have done, but I did the opposite to get what I wanted. And even though I felt guilty that I deceived my friend, I never did anything to remedy the situation. I chose evil instead of goodness. This particular event happened close to fifty years ago, but I still feel embarrassed about it.

WHY WE FAIL AT GOODNESS

How could I go to church each week, hear the Gospel, and still do something that I knew was wrong? The *Catechism* gives us some insight into this:

By his reason, man recognizes the voice of God which urges him "to do what is good and avoid what is evil." Everyone is obliged to follow this law, which makes itself heard in conscience and is fulfilled in the love of God and of neighbor. Living a moral life bears witness to the dignity of the person. "Man, enticed by the Evil One, abused his freedom at the very beginning of history." He succumbed to temptation and did what was evil. He still desires the good, but his nature bears the wound of original sin. He is now inclined to evil and subject to error. (*CCC* 1706–1707)

WILL YOU CHOOSE TO BE LIGHT?

You and I choose between good and evil multiple times each day and will continue to do so for the rest of our lives. And, while I can be fairly certain that I won't deliberately cheat someone again as I did in the postage stamp incident, there will be times when I will choose evil over goodness.

Choosing evil doesn't always have to be blatant. It can be as subtle as gossiping about a boss, coworker, priest, or teacher. It can involve gesturing rudely to a fellow driver as you rush to get to work or posting nasty comments on social media. We can choose evil by tuning in to a scandalous TV program or visiting certain websites. To complicate matters even more, evil often looks very appealing.

So what can we do to address this dilemma? If we're not careful, we can easily lapse into believing that only God is good and that we can never practice goodness on a regular basis. To borrow a phrase popularized by Alcoholics Anonymous, that is an example of "stinkin' thinkin'"! You were created by God in his image and likeness. And, since everything he creates is good, *you are good*. No matter how many bad things you have done in your life, you are not a bad person. Please remember that. With the help of the Holy Spirit, you can turn around your life and become a light shining in the darkness. If you don't believe me, listen to Jesus: "You are the light of the world. A city set on a mountain cannot be hidden. Nor do they light a lamp and then put it under a bushel basket; it is set on a lampstand, where it gives light to all in the house. Just so, your light must shine before others, that they may see your good deeds and glorify your heavenly Father" (Mt 5:14–16).

You are the light of the world. It's not up to the other guy. It's up to *you* to be a light to those around you. Notice that Jesus didn't exclude anyone in making this proclamation. That means that all of us are capable of doing good. That news alone should make us feel great.

Now, here's the really cool part: When we perform good works in a visible way, it gives others the opportunity to give glory to God. Of course, Jesus isn't telling us to do good so that people will think highly of us. Rather, he is emphasizing the importance of being a positive witness.

A WORD OF CAUTION

I feel that I should mention something serious here. Because you are capable of doing good and leading others to the Lord, you have a huge target on your back. I'm telling you this not to scare you but to make you aware. Satan will do everything in his power to convince you that you're a bad person and incapable of doing anything good. He knows that if he can get you to believe this lie, there is an excellent chance that you will stop trying to practice goodness. When that happens, your positive witness disappears as well. This can have the effect of not only putting distance between you and the Lord but depriving others of growing close to him as well.

Be careful! When St. Peter writes that "your opponent the devil is prowling around like a roaring lion looking for someone to devour" (1 Pt 5:8), he isn't kidding. Satan can't force you to do anything, but he can lie to you and sound convincing. Don't listen to him. Yesterday is gone. If you did something evil in the past, go to Confession and stop carrying around the extra baggage. You were created to be a saint. With God's grace, it is possible.

As proof that there is hope for you and me, remember that many of God's chosen instruments had nefarious pasts. Abraham, Jacob, Moses, David, Peter, and Paul all did bad things at one time or another. Some of their failings were worse than others, but they were all sinners. That didn't stop God from choosing them to do his work. Like us, they were given the opportunity to repent and start over. They weren't suddenly made perfect, but were given the grace to carry out their God-given missions. By cooperating with God's grace, they went on to perform many great works of holiness. We are each called to a similar mission, made possible only by God's grace and the working of the Holy Spirit.

ADVICE FROM A PROPHET

Now that you know you have what it takes to let the Holy Spirit's goodness flow through you, let's look at ways to put this into practice. The prophet Micah gives us some great ideas on how to get started: "You have been told, O mortal, what is good, and what the LORD requires of you: Only to do justice and to love goodness, and to walk humbly with your God" (6:8, RSVCE). As this Bible verse declares, God has shown us what it means to be good. By his words and actions, Jesus gives us the ultimate example of goodness. We can imitate him by doing justice, loving goodness, and walking humbly with God. Let's explore each of these ways of practicing goodness.

- *Do justice.* There is much injustice in the world today. The poor and vulnerable are frequently deprived of the dignity due to them as children of God. People are lifted up for what they accomplish rather than for who they are. Millions of individuals around the world lack access to basic needs such as food, water, and shelter. Unborn babies and the medically vulnerable are legally murdered every day through abortion and euthanasia.

  We frequently walk by or ignore those who are homeless. Sometimes we even blame God for allowing this injustice to exist. Why doesn't he do something about poverty and all the injustice in the world? I can't speak for God, but it's entirely possible that he wants *us* to do something about it. We can pray for an end to abortion and speak out against it whenever possible, vote for pro-life candidates, contribute to organizations that feed the hungry or provide shelter to the homeless, and treat all people (regardless of race, occupation, or social standing) with equal dignity.

- *Love goodness.* In the previous chapter, we discussed kindness and how it is closely tied to mercy. When we are merciful to others, we imitate the Lord. But what does it mean to *love* kindness or mercy? To love kindness means that we are passionate about putting it into practice. We want to do more than just check the box and fulfill our obligation. When we love kindness, we actively look for opportunities to show mercy to those around us.

    Loving kindness is different from forcing yourself to be kind and merciful. You do it because you want to and not because you have to. How do we get to the point where we have a strong desire to be merciful to others? As we have discussed, it starts by recognizing how merciful God has been to us. We can then pray that he will change our desires so that we truly care about paying that mercy forward. In addition, we can pray for the grace to be humble so that we will yield to the promptings of the Holy Spirit.

- *Walk humbly with God.* One of the main reasons we fail to produce the fruit of goodness is that we lack humility. Even though the goodness of the Holy Spirit lives in us, he will not violate our free will. If we don't want to be good (or kind or loving or joyful, etc.), he will not force us to be so. In all honesty, there are times when I don't feel like letting the gifts of the Spirit flow through me. Even though the Lord is all-powerful, he gives me the final say. Why would I want to stop the Spirit from working in my life? The main reason is pride. It takes humility to love someone when they are mean to us, to be joyful when we feel miserable, and to show mercy when we believe someone doesn't deserve it. We need to pray for this kind of humility and the grace to put it into practice.

Let me once again remind you that it is possible for you to practice God's goodness in your daily life. The fact that you may have done bad things doesn't make you a bad person. You are created in God's image and likeness, and that makes you good. Don't forget it!

REMEMBER

1. You are created in God's image and likeness. Therefore, you are good.

2. The fact that you have done bad things does not make you a bad person.

3. Letting others see your good works gives them the opportunity to give glory to God.

4. Satan wants you to believe that you are not capable of doing good. He will call attention to all the bad things you have done in the past. He is a liar. Don't listen to him!

5. You can practice goodness by doing justice, loving goodness, and walking humbly with God.

REFLECT

1. Do you ever think of yourself or others as bad? Why?

2. Whom do you think of as being good? God, the saints, yourself, others?

3. Do you sometimes think that you can't be good? Why or why not?

4. Name some specific ways you can let the goodness of the Holy Spirit flow through you today.

5. How can a lack of humility prevent you from doing good things?

RESPOND

Practice goodness today by posting only positive comments on social media, avoiding gossip, making a charitable contribution, or praying for someone.

LET'S PRAY

Dear Holy Spirit, sometimes I feel that only you, the saints, and the angels can be good. I know that this is not true. Help me to be humble enough to let you work through me. By doing this, I hope to give glory to my heavenly Father. Amen.

10

Faithfulness

Praise the Lord, all you nations! Extol him, all you peoples! His mercy for us is strong; the faithfulness of the Lord is forever. Hallelujah!
—Psalm 117

How does it feel when someone promises us something and doesn't deliver? We may feel angry, disappointed, or heartbroken. The fact that we have been let down by others (hundreds of times) doesn't make it any easier to take. So what can we do?

In this chapter, we will focus on God as the ultimate example of faithfulness. He is always good for his word and always follows through. With the help of the Holy Spirit, we too can be faithful to God and those around us.

Let's first address something you already know. People sometimes break promises. The mechanic assures you that your car will be ready in an hour, and you're still waiting to hear from him three hours later. Your son promises that he will take out the trash, and it doesn't happen. A friend offers to go to a concert with you and backs out at the last minute. Marital infidelity, political corruption, and other forms of betrayal occur on a regular basis. The fact that people behave in this way should not come as a surprise.

While some offenses are more serious than others, they all stem from our fallen human nature. Making a promise is easier than following through. People will let you down from time to time. Sometimes they don't even realize what they are doing. Therefore, don't be devastated if someone makes a promise to you and doesn't deliver. It happens. Not only will people go back on their word to you, but they also will do it to God.

The Bible gives us many instances of people's faithlessness to God. Throughout salvation history, the Israelites repeatedly broke their covenant with the Lord. Even though the circumstances were different each time it happened, the basic pattern was always the same. When they experienced difficulties and suffering, they cried out to God for help and were more than willing to do what he asked of them. Then, once things turned around for them, they lost interest in obeying the Lord and resumed idol worship. They were faithful to God only as long as there was something in it for them. After he delivered them from the crisis du jour and their troubles disappeared, they forgot all about the promises they made to him. As a result, the Lord often had to allow trials to occur in the lives of his people. This would get their attention, and they would repent. Before too long, however, they would be back to their old tricks and the cycle would repeat. Never learning from past history, the Chosen People would continually fail to be faithful to the Lord.

GOD IS FAITHFUL (EVEN WHEN WE'RE NOT!)

On the other hand, God is faithful and always keeps his promises. And, for the record, he's made a lot of promises. (If you don't believe me, google it.) While I can't give you an exact number, I can highlight some Bible verses that illustrate my point.

- "Not a single word of the blessing that the LORD had promised to the house of Israel failed; it all came true" (Jos 21:45).

- "The LORD is trustworthy in all his words, and loving in all his works" (Ps 145:13).

- "God is faithful, and by him you were called to fellowship with his Son, Jesus Christ our Lord" (1 Cor 1:9).

- "Let us hold unwaveringly to our confession that gives us hope, for he who made the promise is trustworthy" (Heb 10:23).

We can rest assured that the Lord has fulfilled (or is in the process of fulfilling) all of the promises he made in the Bible. He can be trusted and will never let us down. God is faithful and always keeps his promises.

HOW FAITHFUL ARE YOU?

Now it's time for the really tough question: How faithful are you to God and to others? It's a question I ask myself, too.

When I was younger, I was terrible about keeping my promises. My friend Ray was often on the receiving end of this bad habit. Here's how it would work. I would tell Ray that I would go to some event with him (a Catholic singles group, a prayer meeting, dinner), and then I'd change my mind at the last minute. I was so self-centered that I never even thought it was unfair to him.

One day, he called me on it and let me know that I was being a jerk. After getting angry and telling him I didn't care (thus proving his point!), I gave it some thought and realized that he was right. It sounds so basic, but this was a real eye-opener for me, and I'm grateful that he let me know.

In addition to Ray and many others, I frequently broke my promises to God. Through the years, I often reneged on my pledge to pray regularly (usually after the Lord delivered me from a crisis), do more spiritual reading, or avoid my "favorite" sins. The Lord was extremely patient with me. It took many years of treating him unfairly before he spoke to me through a Bible verse. Like Ray's admonition, this message hit me like a ton of bricks and helped me to become more faithful to God: "You say, 'The LORD's way is not fair!' Hear now, house of Israel: Is it my way that is unfair? Are not your ways unfair?" (Ez 18:25).

STEPS TO FAITHFULNESS

When we discussed the fruit of patience, I made the point that it's not about you. The one thing I want you to remember when it comes to faithfulness is that it *is* about you! God is faithful, and that will never change. We don't have to worry about him. And we must accept that there will always be other people who will break their promises to us. We can bring it to their attention (as Ray did with me), but we can't control their behavior. What we can do, with the help of the Holy Spirit, is become more faithful to God and those around us. If we all commit to doing so, the world will be a better place.

Do you want to become a more faithful person? Are you willing to change? Once I realized that my lack of faithfulness was hurting Jesus and others, I wanted to change. Having that desire is an important first step. But as with any of the virtues, growing in faithfulness can be painful because it requires work and persistence. Even though the Holy Spirit will do most of the work (if you ask him), there will be times when you won't want to follow through on your promises. Here are a few tips that will help you to succeed.

- *Make realistic promises.* One of the main reasons we fail to honor our commitments to God and others is that we make unrealistic promises. Pledging to read the Bible for two hours daily or to pray every hour on the hour will probably not work for most people. If you're not used to praying or reading the Bible, five or ten minutes daily is a good place to start. Committing to daily prayer or Bible reading is challenging enough. Don't make it more difficult than it has to be.

- *Recognize that your words have meaning.* Sometimes we forget that our words actually mean something. According to Jesus, "on the day of judgment people will render an account for every careless word they speak. By your words you will be acquitted, and by your words you will be condemned" (Mt 12:36–37). We should get into the habit of listening to what we say. Don't say it unless you really mean it!

- *Take your time before promising.* I have learned to pause before I make a commitment. Do I really have the time? Can I follow through? Is this a good idea? You will be amazed what a difference this practice can make. Get into the habit of turning to the Holy Spirit before promising anything. Ask him to guide your thoughts and let you know what to do. It's much better to take your time and avoid making an unrealistic promise than committing to something and going back on your word.

- *Learn to say no.* You can't say yes to everything. Nothing will burn you out faster than volunteering at every school event and helping everyone who asks for your assistance. Understanding your limitations is a good thing. If you don't learn to do it, you'll spread yourself too thin and will not be able to follow through on your promises. The Holy Spirit often speaks through our bodies. If you're too tired, just say no!

- *Remember that faithfulness pleases God.* When we are faithful to our word, God is pleased. In the book of Proverbs, we're told that "lying lips are an abomination to the LORD, but those who are truthful, his delight" (12:22). It never occurred to me to wonder what God thought when I was breaking my promises left and right. This verse is a powerful reminder of the fact that the Lord cares about the decisions we make.

- *Imitate Jesus.* Love of comfort is another reason we sometimes fail to be faithful. It's easy to commit verbally, but it takes effort to follow through. How many times have you agreed to do something (help a friend move, go to an event at church, wake up early to pray) but changed your mind when the day arrived? What sounded like a good idea three weeks ago suddenly seems unbearable.

NO PAIN, NO GAIN

Here's the problem: Being faithful is often uncomfortable or even painful. More often than not, it doesn't *feel* good. Because I enjoy comfort, this has been a constant struggle for me. I have found it helpful to think about the life of Jesus, especially his passion. He could have backed out of the plan once it got too painful, but he didn't. When challenged to come down from the Cross (see Mk 15:30), he stayed put because it was the right thing to do. After meditating on the Stations of the Cross or the Sorrowful Mysteries of the Rosary, I usually find that going to that party doesn't seem so bad—even if I'm tired.

It's easy to get into the habit of making promises and not following through. People do it all the time. As Christians, however, we need to do better. We are called to imitate Christ, who was faithful to the end. It is possible, but it requires work. As with any of the fruits, we need to get out of the way and let the Holy Spirit operate in us. Our life on earth is relatively short. As we approach the finish line, our goal should be to proclaim with St. Paul: "For I am already being poured out like a libation, and the time of my departure is at hand. I have

competed well; I have finished the race; I have kept the faith"
(2 Tm 4:6–7).

REMEMBER

1. God is faithful and always keeps his promises.

2. Don't be surprised when people go back on their word.

3. One of the main reasons we fail to honor our commitments to God and others is that we make unrealistic promises. Take your time and think before you make a promise.

4. Words have meaning. Don't say anything that you don't mean.

5. When it comes to faithfulness, Jesus should be our role model. He suffered greatly but never abandoned his mission.

REFLECT

1. Think of a time when someone broke a promise made to you. How did it feel?

2. Think of a time when you did not follow through after making a promise to God or others. What caused you to go back on your word?

3. Picture what it would be like if the faithfulness of the Holy Spirit was active in your life. Ask for his help.

4. How do you think Jesus feels when you break a promise to him or someone else?

5. Picture yourself standing before the Lord on the day of your judgment. He wants to discuss your faithfulness. How do you feel? What can you do now to be better prepared for that day?

RESPOND

Make a promise to God that you will do something concrete for him every day for a week (read the Bible, pray, go to daily Mass) and then stick to it. (Hint: Remember to be realistic with your promise. Ten minutes of daily Bible reading is more doable than an hour.)

LET'S PRAY

Dear Jesus, you faithfully carried your cross and endured suffering because it was your Father's will. Please help me to be faithful. I have tried many times and failed. With your help, however, I know I can be successful. In your name I pray. Amen.

11

Gentleness

Take my yoke upon you, and learn from me, for I
am gentle and lowly of heart, and you will find rest
for your souls.
—Matthew 11:29, RSVCE

Typically, we don't associate gentleness with power. In reality,
however, it is impossible to be gentle without being powerful.
Gentleness can best be described as power under control.
According to St. Francis de Sales, "Nothing is so strong as
gentleness, nothing so gentle as real strength."[8] Jesus had the
power to calm storms, cast out demons, and raise the dead,
yet he described himself as being gentle. That is because gentleness is rooted in strength.

When writing about the fruit of gentleness, St. Paul
uses the Greek word *praytes,* which can also be translated
as "meekness." It should not be confused with weakness. A
truly gentle person is powerful but knows how to channel that
power and use it for good. Realizing that he was nearing the
end of his life, Paul wrote to his younger colleague, Timothy,
encouraging him to proclaim the truth with gentleness: "A
slave of the Lord should not quarrel, but should be gentle with

everyone, able to teach, tolerant, correcting opponents with kindness" (2 Tm 2:24–25).

Nobody had more power than Jesus, yet he never misused it. He corrected people with gentleness. He was forceful at times, especially with the Pharisees and Sadducees, but only when necessary. If we truly want the Holy Spirit to work through us, we should have the same mindset.

I have to admit that I have struggled with this. After my conversion, I felt empowered by my newfound knowledge of the Catholic faith and looked for occasions to share it with others. I knew—and I wanted everyone else to know—that the Catholic Church had the fullness of truth. Unfortunately, my approach often consisted of seeking out those who were "wrong" and setting them straight. I looked for liturgical abuses at Mass, searched for misinformation on Catholic internet forums, and scoured my diocesan newspaper for potentially heretical comments. With all the subtlety of a bulldozer, I proceeded to write letters, post comments, and make phone calls. Although I wasn't overtly offensive, I'm sure I came across as pompous and arrogant. My approach was not very gentle. It also wasn't very effective.

THE GENTLE EVANGELIST?

Paul wasn't the only apostle to encourage gentleness in evangelization. After proclaiming the importance of sharing the faith with others, St. Peter went on to emphasize the need for gentleness and reverence: "Always be ready to give an explanation to anyone who asks you for a reason for your hope, but do it with gentleness and reverence, keeping your conscience clear, so that, when you are maligned, those who defame your good conduct in Christ may themselves be put to shame" (1 Pt 3:15–16). As Catholic Christians, we are called to share the Good News with those around us. Peter, the first pope, understood this, and that's why he included this message in his letter. Because he lived in a time of great religious persecution, however, he also realized that not everyone would be happy to hear the Gospel of Jesus Christ. Therefore, he stressed the need for gentleness and reverence.

In a time of persecution it made sense for early Christians to take a gentle approach when sharing Christ with those who did not know him. And yet we are wise to use a similar approach, rather than yelling at or belittling those who push back on our message. Trust me on this one. It can be very easy to cross the line from evangelization to sin. Be careful!

Always remember that the Holy Spirit is ultimately in charge of your efforts to evangelize. You may have an incredibly logical, fact-based, and seemingly irrefutable reason why someone should embrace the teaching of the Catholic Church, but it can still be rejected. Until that person's heart is opened by the Holy Spirit, your words will fall on deaf ears. And, while that can sound discouraging, it actually removes the pressure. Your job is to follow the lead of the Holy Spirit and share the Gospel with gentleness and reverence. That's it! The rest is up to the Spirit.

Don't let your frustration boil over into anger or other kinds of sin. If you are rejected after sharing the message, it's time to move on. You did what you were supposed to do. Continue to pray for that person and wait for the Lord to reopen the door if and when he desires. Very often, you will be planting the seeds and someone else will be sent to reap the harvest. Whenever you evangelize, pray for the grace to surrender to the Holy Spirit's leadership. Doing so can help you to better understand your role and stay out of trouble. It can also lead to greater success in winning souls for Christ.

GENTLE HUMILITY

Do you remember when the mother of James and John approached Jesus (see Matthew 20:20–24) and attempted to secure top positions for her sons in the kingdom? It was clear that she misunderstood the nature of the kingdom, but she was not alone. Overhearing the conversation, the other apostles felt they were missing out and grew angry at the two brothers. Everybody missed the point!

Jesus used the opportunity to instruct them: "You know that the rulers of the Gentiles lord it over them, and the great ones make their authority over them felt. But it shall not be so among you. Rather, whoever wishes to be great among you shall be your servant; whoever wishes to be first among you shall be your slave. Just so, the Son of Man did not come to be served but to serve and to give his life as a ransom for many" (Mt 20:25–28).

With power comes the opportunity to be gentle. Even though he was God, Jesus "did not regard equality with God something to be grasped. Rather, he emptied himself, taking the form of a slave" (Phil 2:6–7) and willingly submitted to dying on the Cross. He didn't do that because he was weak; he did it because he was powerful. Great power provides an opportunity for even greater gentleness.

OPPORTUNITIES FOR GENTLENESS

Evangelization is not the only activity in which we should practice gentleness. There are plenty of everyday encounters that give us a chance to display this powerful fruit of the Holy Spirit. Here are a few examples:

- *In family life.* Members of a family have many occasions to practice gentleness on a regular basis. As a husband, I can choose to let my wife have the last word in an argument, or accept criticism with humility. Children can choose to obey their parents without grumbling. Parents can avoid saying "I told you so" to their children and can correct them lovingly without excessive commentary. If you are open to finding them, you will notice many situations where you can choose to be gentle.

- *In the marketplace.* Think of the last time you received poor customer service—the waiter got your order wrong, or the clerk handling returns moved too slowly. In such situations, you can mutter sarcastically (or worse), or you can smile and look pleasant. When you decide to speak up, bear in mind that sarcasm and gentleness are incompatible.

  What if you work in a customer service position? Even when you can't give the customer what he or she wants, you can always practice gentleness by acknowledging the customer's concerns and desires, choosing words to soften the blow rather than shrugging off the situation with a "that's the way it is" attitude.

- *In the workplace.* Employers, managers, and employees all have daily opportunities to display gentleness in the workplace. In my career in the corporate world, I have been treated both gently and harshly by management. One particular incident stands out in my mind.

  While in high school, I worked part time as a cashier in a variety store during the Christmas season. One Friday evening, when I had a very long line, my cash drawer somehow got jammed shut. I'm not sure what caused the problem, but I was forced to contact my supervisor, who tried unsuccessfully to open the drawer. Despite the unhappy line of customers, she remained calm, didn't lecture me, and called the store manager. All I remember about him is that he was tall, always wore a suit, and never smiled. I panicked internally as he worked on prying open the drawer without saying a word.

  In a few minutes he was successful, and I was back in business. Without making eye contact or asking me what happened, he snapped, "Wake up!" and walked away. This incident occurred forty years ago, but I can still remember feeling empty, scared, and incompetent for the remainder of my time working at the store. This was the first and only time he ever spoke to me, but I'll never forget how awful I felt. A little gentleness can make a big difference in someone's life.

- *On social media.* There is a serious shortage of gentleness on social media. No matter how "right" you are or how "wrong" the other person is, it's always wise to pause before you post. Your comments, even if they are justified, can do a lot of damage.

Before you post a comment, ask the Holy Spirit if it can actually help someone—and if it is written with charity, gentleness, and reverence. If not, delete it and back away from the computer (you'd be surprised how often I have to do this). Even if it's a member of the clergy or other public figure, use discretion as much for your own sake as theirs. Follow the example of St. Paul (see Ephesians 4:29) and St. Peter (see 1 Peter 3:15), and let gentleness season your online interactions.

- *While driving.* How does it feel when someone is tailgating you even though you're driving at the speed limit? What about those times when you're trying to merge into traffic and nobody lets you in? You are in control of your vehicle and can choose to drive gently. You can practice by giving the slowpoke in front of you some room or by letting in the jerk who waited until the last moment to merge into the construction traffic. These deliberate attempts to practice gentleness may seem small to you, but not to the Lord.

Every day, we have countless opportunities to treat others with gentleness. The more we follow the Holy Spirit's lead and put this fruit into practice, the easier it will be for us to recognize these occasions as they arise. The other day I was in the grocery store standing in a long line. The woman in front of me had a full cart, and I had only five items. No other cashiers were available, so there wasn't much I could do. I was determined to settle in and be patient. Suddenly, the woman turned around and asked me if I'd like to go ahead of her. She had the power to remain ahead of me, but she chose to allow me to go first. Her act of gentleness resulted in our having a nice conversation.

Always remember that gentleness doesn't mean powerlessness. As a baptized Christian, you have the full power of the Holy Spirit dwelling in you. How you use that power is up to you. In 1 Kings 19:11–13, the Lord told Elijah to stand on the mountain and wait for him to pass by. The prophet obeyed and waited as a great and powerful wind tore apart the rocks. The Lord wasn't in the wind. Then came an earthquake, but still no Lord. The earthquake was followed by a fire, but still no sign of God. Finally, Almighty God appeared to Elijah in a "still, small voice" (v. 12, RSVCE).

Nothing is more powerful than letting the gentleness of the Holy Spirit flow through you. That's exactly what Jesus did.

REMEMBER

1. Gentleness can be described as power under control.

2. Meekness is not the same thing as weakness.

3. Without gentleness, your evangelization attempts will be ineffective.

4. We can practice gentleness in many situations—in family life, at the grocery store, in the workplace, on social media, and even when driving.

5. Almighty God appeared to the prophet Elijah not in a powerful wind, earthquake, or fire but in a gentle whisper. The ultimate display of power is gentleness.

REFLECT

1. Who is the gentlest person you know? Why?
2. How has God been gentle with you? Be specific.
3. List some examples of how you can practice gentleness in your daily life.
4. What is the world's opinion on gentleness and power? How does that differ from the Christian philosophy?
5. Why is it so difficult to be gentle?

RESPOND

Be gentle with someone today on the internet, in the store, at home, or on the phone. Ask a cashier or waiter how their day is going. Let another driver merge ahead of you in traffic. Purposely avoid getting the last word in an argument.

LET'S PRAY

Dear Holy Spirit, help me to practice gentleness in my daily life. When I am tempted to use my power to get my way or control others, remind me of how Jesus lived and grant me the grace to follow your lead. In Jesus' name I pray. Amen.

12

Self-Control

A man without self-control
is like a city broken into and left without walls.
—Proverbs 25:28, RSVCE

Throughout this book, we have been discussing the fruits of the Spirit in the order they are listed in Galatians 5:22–23. I find it very appropriate that the last fruit we will examine is self-control because, in a sense, this entire book has been about *controlling our desire to block the Holy Spirit from working in us.*

The idea of standing in the way of the Holy Spirit seems like insanity, but most of us do it several times each day. Our fallen human nature constantly influences us to choose what we want over what God wants. With the help of the Holy Spirit and some willpower, however, we can overcome this tendency and learn to control our passions.

On the night before he died, Jesus asked Peter, James, and John to accompany him as he prayed in the garden of Gethsemane (Mt 26:36–46). He was counting on his closest friends to remain with him in his hour of need. Telling the three apostles about the great sorrow in his heart, Jesus asked them to sit there and stay awake with him as he prayed to his Father.

It sounds like a simple request, but they couldn't handle it. After falling on his face in intense prayer, Jesus returned and discovered them *asleep*. Can you imagine how disappointed he must have been? It's not as though Jesus asked them to do something difficult. All they were asked to do was sit with him and stay awake. The Lord's words to Peter are direct and contain a valuable lesson: "So you could not keep watch with me for one hour? Watch and pray that you may not undergo the test. The spirit is willing, but the flesh is weak" (Mt 26:40–41).

Now, if you've ever been in a frightening situation, you know how comforting it can be to have a supportive friend stand with you. And no doubt the three apostles had every intention of staying awake. And yet their tiredness got the best of them. At some point, sleep was more desirable than keeping Jesus company, and they gave in to that desire.

Like Peter, James, and John, we often fail to control our actions, choosing instant gratification over self-denial. And yet, if we look closely at this scripture passage, we will see that Jesus reprimands the apostles not for falling asleep but for their *failure to pray for the strength to overcome temptation*.

THE GIFT OF VIGILANCE

Laziness is a real (and potentially dangerous) threat. Falling asleep while you're saying your prayers isn't a sin, but it could be a sign that you have your priorities wrong. For many years, I used to squeeze God into my schedule at the end of the day. After doing all the "important" things that pleased me,

I managed to pray for a few minutes as I drifted off to sleep. The problem wasn't that I was falling asleep while praying but that I was putting God last in my life.

Before you begin to worry about the "spirit is willing, but the flesh is weak" message, let's focus on the recommendation Jesus makes to the sleepy apostles. Note that he urges Peter, James, and John to "watch and pray"—that is, to be vigilant. Like them, we can overcome our drive to seek pleasure (often in the wrong things) if we remain alert to temptations and overcome them by leaning not on our own strength but on the graces God gives us if we ask.

Satan hates it when we rely on God in this way; he loves to use our weakness to lure us into sin. He expertly stages sin so it looks appealing. If it didn't, there would be no threat. Becoming aware of this is half the battle.

ASKING FOR HELP

In addition to vigilance, Jesus recommends prayer as part of the game plan for the disciples. We'd be wise to pay attention to his advice. When it comes to self-control, nothing trips us up more than failing to ask for help. Trying to control our desires by willpower alone will only result in failure and frustration. It might work temporarily, but not for long. With the Lord's help, however, we can overcome any temptation we encounter. According to St. Paul, "God is faithful and will not let you be tried beyond your strength; but with the trial he will also provide a way out, so that you may be able to bear it" (1 Cor 10:13).

The apostles are prime examples of individuals whose lives were transformed when they received the fruit of self-control. They are often called out for their imperfections. Looking at their missteps can make us feel better about our own failures. But here's something that rarely gets mentioned: The apostles didn't receive the Holy Spirit until after Jesus rose from the dead (see John 20:22). Therefore, it's understandable that they messed up so many times before that. Once they received the Holy Spirit, their lives changed dramatically. In addition to what we read in the Acts of the Apostles and the letters of St. Paul, tradition holds that (with the exception of John and Judas), they died as martyrs. Amazing!

WE ARE FULL OF THE SPIRIT OF JESUS

Without a doubt, the best possible example of self-control can be found in Jesus Christ. The entire life of Jesus is an illustration of perfect self-control. He was obedient to his parents (Lk 2:51), resisted the temptations of Satan (Mt 4:1–11), refused to back down from Pontius Pilate (Jn 19:8–11), and ignored the taunts of the chief priests and scribes when they urged him to come down from the Cross (Mk 15:31–32). The words of the prophet Isaiah give us insight into the powerful self-control possessed by the Lord: "Though harshly treated, he submitted and did not open his mouth; like a lamb led to slaughter or a sheep silent before shearers, he did not open his mouth" (Is 53:7).

We may assume that as humans we cannot exercise that same degree of self-control. Wrong! Jesus was guided by the Holy Spirit. Several times in the New Testament (Acts 16:7;

Phil 1:19; Rom 8:9; 1 Pt 1:11), the Holy Spirit is referred to as the "Spirit of Jesus" or the "Spirit of Christ." We can clearly see all of the Spirit's fruits (including self-control) when we examine the life of Jesus.

Here's the best part: The Spirit of Jesus—the incredible power that enabled Jesus to fulfill his earthly mission—comes to live in you through the sacraments of Baptism and Confirmation. As hard as it may be to believe, you can exhibit the same self-control shown by Jesus. Let that sink in for a minute. Mind-boggling, isn't it? It's also 100 percent true. Never underestimate what the Holy Spirit can do in your life.

As we've discussed, this involves inviting the Spirit to work through you and then getting out of the way. It sounds simple, but it can be extremely difficult to put into practice. When you really want to give someone a piece of your mind or give in to a sinful pleasure, you may not care what the Holy Spirit has to say.

I want to be completely honest about something. Self-control does not come naturally to me. It's not easy for me to control myself at all-you-can-eat buffets or when I have a full box of doughnuts in front of me. I haven't smoked a cigarette in over twenty years, but it took many attempts before I was finally able to quit. Controlling my tongue (especially when it comes to sarcasm) has been a challenge throughout my life. I could give you many more examples, but I think you get the point. Let's just say that I'm very familiar with being unable to control my passions. Despite having that weakness, I have learned a few tricks along the way. If you struggle with self-control, you may find them helpful.

- *Focus on the big picture.* We should always remember that the main purpose of practicing self-control is to imitate Jesus and to make it to heaven. There will be times when we desperately want something that isn't good for us. It may be a box of candy, but it could also be something immoral or illegal. Our desire for pleasure is often stronger than our desire to do the right thing. Keeping our focus on Jesus is not foolproof, but it can definitely help. Listen to his words: "Whoever wishes to come after me must deny himself, take up his cross, and follow me. For whoever wishes to save his life will lose it, but whoever loses his life for my sake and that of the gospel will save it. What profit is there for one to gain the whole world and forfeit his life?" (Mark 8:34–36).

  Pleasure should never be the main goal of our lives. We should be focused on following Jesus and getting to heaven. Unless we learn to practice self-denial and control our passions, we're not going to achieve the ultimate goal.

- *Learn from the past.* I can't tell you how many times I've regretted opening my mouth when I should have remained silent. In just about every instance, I ignored the gentle voice of the Holy Spirit urging me to control my tongue. Even though I knew what I was about to say was wrong, I did it anyway. Over the course of my life, I have hurt many people with my words and felt bad about doing so. Even though I have confessed these sins and know that I've been forgiven, I don't allow myself to forget completely. Why? It helps me to remember that failing to control my words (and actions) has consequences.

- *Practice self-denial.* Every day we have many opportunities to deny ourselves in some way. We can get out of bed as soon as the alarm clock rings, have one less cookie for dessert, or perform small acts of kindness for family members. Learning to deny ourselves in small ways will help us succeed when the big things arise. Saying no to a doughnut might not directly affect my salvation, but it strengthens my self-control muscles. That could be extremely beneficial one day.

DON'T GET DISCOURAGED

None of us should get discouraged when we fail. It not only *can* happen but also *will* happen. Although he never sinned or lost self-control, Jesus fell three times while carrying his cross. One of my favorite devotional booklets for meditating on the Passion is *Everyone's Way of the Cross*, by Clarence Enzler. Here is the meditation for the ninth station (Jesus Falls the Third Time). It's written as a joint dialogue between Christ and the reader.

> *Christ speaks*: Completely drained of strength I lie, collapsed upon the cobblestones. My body cannot move. No blows, no kicks, can rouse it up. And yet my will is mine. And so is yours. Know this, my other self, your body may be broken, but no force on earth and none in hell can take away your will. Your will is yours.

> *I reply:* My Lord, I see you take a moment's rest
> then rise and stagger on. So I can do because my
> will is mine. When all my strength is gone and
> guilt and self-reproach press me to earth and
> seem to hold me fast, protect me from the sin of
> Judas—save me from despair! Lord, never let me
> feel that any sin of mine is greater than your love.
> No matter what my past has been I can begin
> anew.[9]

As a man, Jesus subjected himself to the weakness of the
human body. Because he fell (not by sinning but because
of physical exhaustion) while carrying out his mission, he
reminds me that I too will fall. His actions also teach me a
greater lesson: Each time he fell, Jesus got back on his feet.
That's the takeaway. The Holy Spirit does the bulk of the work,
but it's still a matter of the will. When you fail to control your
passions, get back up and pray for the grace to do better next
time. No matter how often you fall, never stop trying.

REMEMBER

1. Self-control is a matter of controlling our desires and
   letting the Holy Spirit work through us.

2. Our fallen human nature constantly influences us to
   choose what we want over what God wants.

3. One of the main reasons we fail to control our desires is
   that we don't pray for God's assistance.

4. "God is faithful and will not let you be tried beyond your strength; but with the trial he will also provide a way out, so that you may be able to bear it" (1 Cor 10:13).

5. When you fail to control your passions, don't lose hope. Instead, get back up and pray for the grace to do better next time.

REFLECT

1. Name some specific situations in which you struggle to display self-control. Pick the one that most seriously impacts your relationship with the Lord, and pray for the grace to improve.

2. Why do you think it was possible for Jesus to maintain control at all times? Be specific.

3. What steps can you take to improve your self-control?

4. How can improving your self-control benefit others?

5. Can you see any positive benefits that come from those times when you fail to maintain your self-control? (Hint: It has to do with relying on God.)

RESPOND

Deny yourself in some small way today—skip the cream or sugar in your coffee, don't butter your bread or salt your food, have water instead of soda, etc.

LET'S PRAY

Abba Father, through the power of your Holy Spirit, grant me the grace to control my passions in all situations. I ask this in the name of Jesus, your Son. Amen.

Conclusion

So, what do you think? Are you ready to let the Holy Spirit transform you to be more like Christ, so that you can display love, joy, peace, patience, kindness, goodness, faithfulness, gentleness, and self-control every day? It sounds daunting, but with the help of the Holy Spirit you can do it.

Don't give in to discouragement, anger, or stress. Don't think you're too weak to live victoriously. Nobody is asking you to do this on your own. Jesus gave you his Holy Spirit to make up for what you lack. As long as you rely on the Spirit's power and get out of his way, you will produce good fruit.

Holiness (or bearing good fruit) is a joint effort between you and the Holy Spirit. After inviting the Spirit to work in your life, you must then be willing to listen to his promptings and act on them. At that point, you have to trust that his power will work through you. That last step may seem difficult, but it will get easier with time. Before long, you will find yourself being able to imitate Jesus, sleeping calmly even while the storm rages around you.

For this crazy world to become a better place, you and I have to get busy. We can't wait for somebody else to get the job done. Jesus is counting on us to be his hands and feet on the earth. He wouldn't ask if he didn't think we were up for it.

I've been praying for you and will continue to do so. I have total confidence in your ability to be transformed by the Holy Spirit. The fact that you read this book assures me that the Spirit is already working in your life. He will continue to do so, as long as you let him. To borrow some words from our friend St. Paul: "I am confident of this, that the one who began a good work in you will continue to complete it until the day of Christ Jesus" (Phil 1:6).

Notes

1. "Pope Francis' Comments and Address at Catholic Charismatic Renewal Convention," June 1, 2014, https://zenit.org/articles/pope-francis-comments-and-address-at-charismatic-renewal-convention/.

2. For more details, contact the charismatic prayer group at your parish and ask about the Life in the Spirit seminars. If your parish doesn't have a charismatic prayer group, chances are that a nearby parish does.

3. Don Basham, *A Handbook on Holy Spirit Baptism* (New Kensington, PA: Whitaker House, 1969), 152.

4. *Summa Theologica*, I–II, 26 4.

5. Donald Attwater, ed., *A Catholic Dictionary*, 2nd ed., rev. (New York: Macmillan, 1949), 375.

6. Rick Warren, *The Purpose-Driven Life: What on Earth Am I Here For?* (Grand Rapids, MI: Zondervan, 2002), 17.

7. St. Maria Faustina Kowalska, *Diary: Divine Mercy in My Soul* (Stockbridge, MA: Congregation of Marians, 1987), 420.

8. Thomas F. Dailey, O.S.F.S., *Live Today Well: St. Francis de Sales's Simple Approach to Holiness* (Manchester, NH: Sophia Institute Press, 2015), 150.

9. Clarence Enzler, *Everyone's Way of the Cross* (Notre Dame, IN: Ave Maria Press, 2006).

GARY ZIMAK is the bestselling author of several books, including *Give Up Worry for Lent!*, *Stop Worrying and Start Living*, *From Fear to Faith*, *A Worrier's Guide to the Bible*, *Listen to Your Blessed Mother*, *Find a Real Friend in Jesus*, and *Faith, Hope, and Clarity*.

He is the host of *The Gary Zimak Show* and previously served as director of parish services at Mary, Mother of the Redeemer Catholic Church in North Wales, Pennsylvania, and as the host of *Spirit in the Morning* on Holy Spirit Radio in Philadelphia. He is a frequent speaker and retreat leader at Catholic parishes and conferences across the country.

His work has appeared in *Catholic Digest*, the *National Catholic Register*, Catholic Exchange, *Catholic Philly*, and *Catholic Answers Magazine*. Zimak has appeared on numerous television and radio programs, including EWTN's *Bookmark* and *Women of Grace*, *The Jennifer Fulwiler Show*, *Catholic Connection*, *Morning Air*, and the *Son Rise Morning Show*.

Zimak earned a bachelor of science degree in business administration from Drexel University. He lives in Mount Laurel, New Jersey, with his wife. They have two children.

www.FollowingTheTruth.com

Facebook: Gary.Zimak.speaker.author

Twitter: @gary_zimak

ALSO BY
GARY ZIMAK

Give Up Worry for Lent!
40 Days to Finding Peace in Christ

Catholic author and self-described "recovering worrier" Gary Zimak combines practical spirituality, daily scripture readings, and simple action steps to help you kick the worry habit as part of your Lenten renewal. He shows you how to let go of the anxiety-producing areas of your life in order to find the lasting peace that comes from trusting God.

> **"One of the most important Lenten books you'll ever read. Gary Zimak weaves together scripture, personal anecdotes, Church wisdom, and prayer with finesse. Meaty, meaningful, and mighty!"**
>
> —Marge Fenelon
> Author of *Our Lady, Undoer of Knots*